THE ULTIMATE MANIFESTATION BOOK

THE GUIDE TO MANIFESTING YOUR DESIRES AND UNCOVERING THE HIDDEN SECRETS OF THE LAW OF ATTRACTION

DELPHINA WOODS

HENTOPAN
PUBLISHING

© Copyright 2022 Delphina Woods - All rights reserved.

The content contained within this book may not be reproduced, duplicated, or transmitted without direct written permission from the author or the publisher.

Under no circumstances will any blame or legal responsibility be held against the publisher, or author, for any damages, reparation, or monetary loss due to the information contained within this book. Either directly or indirectly.

Legal Notice:

This book is copyright protected. This book is only for personal use. You cannot amend, distribute, sell, use, quote or paraphrase any part, or the content within this book, without the consent of the author or publisher.

Disclaimer Notice:

Please note the information contained within this document is for educational and entertainment purposes only. All effort has been executed to present accurate, up to date, and reliable, complete information. No warranties of any kind are declared or implied. Readers acknowledge that the author is not engaging in the rendering of legal, financial, medical or professional advice. The content within this book has been derived from various sources. Please consult a licensed professional before attempting any techniques outlined in this book.

By reading this document, the reader agrees that under no circumstances is the author responsible for any losses, direct or indirect, which are incurred as a result of the use of the information contained within this document, including, but not limited to, — errors, omissions, or inaccuracies.

CONTENTS

Introduction   v

1. How Does the Law of Attraction Work?   1
2. The Real Reason It Hasn't Worked for You Yet   17
3. Reprogramming Your Subconscious Mind for Manifestation   24
4. Surrender - The SECRET to the Law of Attraction   53
5. Practicing the Law of Attraction   64
6. How Self-Sabotage Reduces the Efficiency of the Law of Attraction   81
7. Living the Law of Attraction   95

Important Law of Attraction Quotes to Live By   107
Conclusion   111

A SPECIAL OFFER

FROM HENTOPAN PUBLISHING

Get this additional book from Delphina Woods just for joining the Hentopan Launch Squad.

Get your free electronic copy by scanning the QR code below with your phone.

INTRODUCTION

We've all heard about the Law of Attraction, but is it real, and can it actually work for you? Imagine being able to manifest your deepest desires and achieve success, wealth, love, and abundance simply by following a few practical daily exercises.

There are 12 spiritual laws that govern all the energy in the universe, and these are called the 12 Universal Laws. The universe exists in perfect harmony with these laws. They are the Laws of Vibration, Attraction, Divine Oneness, Compensation, Polarity, Correspondence, Inspired Action, Cause and Effect, Relativity, Gender, Perpetual Transmutation of Energy and the Law of Rhythm.

So, what exactly is the Law of Attraction? In its simplest form, it's the principle that what you put out into the universe, you attract back. Positivity attracts positivity, and negativity attracts negativity. It's all about believing that your thoughts are part of universal energy and that positive thinking can attract positive outcomes, while negative thinking will bring negative results. In other words, if you believe something to be a certain way, that is what will happen. Your thoughts and feelings are powerful tools that can manifest your deepest desires and amplify your life if used in conjunction with the power of attraction.

The Law of Attraction is more than just imagining something you want and having it magically appear before you. You may have tried to use the Law of Attraction before and given up before you saw any results, dismissing it as something that didn't work for you. The truth is, all things obey the Universal Laws, and the Law of Attraction does work. However, to use it effectively, you need to understand and learn the skills required to put your aspirations into action and know that it takes time for the manifestations to appear.

You see the Law of Attraction in action all around you. People tend to be friends with those who are similar to themselves. Think about your group of friends and why you like being in each other's company. You all had something in common and were drawn to one another. Have you ever bought a new car and then suddenly started seeing that same car everywhere you go? Or been thinking or talking about someone, and the next thing you know, they call or show up unexpectedly? That's the Law of Attraction in action.

You've probably had days where it felt like the world was working against you. You wake up and stub your toe on the way to the bathroom. You're irritated and drip toothpaste on your shirt, which only makes matters worse, and then you spill your coffee, all before you even get out the door to go to work. Now you are late for work because you took an alternative route and got stuck in a traffic jam that you would have otherwise missed. You wouldn't usually have gone that way, but because you were anxious about all the things that happened to make you late, you made a rash decision based on your negative emotions. While it may seem like all these things are merely unfortunate and unconnected incidents, negative energy encourages negative things to happen based on your thoughts and feelings. In just one of those bad moments, a shift from a negative to a positive thought, or even a neutral one, could have caused things to play out differently.

Often, our personal belief that we are not deserving of good things undermines our attempts to achieve happiness. By making and implementing changes to how you view the world around you and adopting a positive outlook, you can shift your pattern of negativity and create healthy and more productive positive patterns instead. Your mindset and perception can change, driven by the techniques used to harness the Law of Attraction, which means you can shift your life from being on a descending path to instead following an upward trajectory.

We all know that one person who always seems to get "lucky." Just as negative thoughts, feelings, and actions attract negative outcomes, the reverse is also true. Think about the attitude this "lucky" individual has and the type of thoughts and feelings they project. Most likely, they view themselves as "lucky" and generally have a positive view of the world around them, thereby attracting positivity and good things.

This is how the Law of Attraction works, and you can make it work for you. Whether or not you are a spiritual person, you are part of the universe, and no matter what you believe, the Universal Laws remain constant.

In *The Manifestation Book* you will learn:

- All about the Law of Attraction
- How the Law of Attraction works
- The basis of the Law of Attraction and why you should believe it
- How to train your subconscious to attract positivity to you

- Habits and beliefs that may make it impossible for the Law of Attraction to work for you
- How to use the Law of Attraction every single day
- The secrets of people who make the Law of Attraction work for them
- And lots more!

1

HOW DOES THE LAW OF ATTRACTION WORK?

The universe is an amazing place bound by specific laws, all working together harmoniously. Whether you are aware of them or not, they all impact your everyday life. The Law of Attraction teaches us that what we put out through our beliefs, actions, thoughts, and feelings will attract those things into our lives, whether positive or negative.

Everything in the universe is made up of energy, vibration, and magnetism. Once you become aware of how things work and apply them in your life, you may be surprised by how much control you have to manifest your future.

THE HISTORY OF THE LAW OF ATTRACTION

The Law of Attraction has been in existence in one form or another since ancient times. Whether it is in Buddhist teachings or Christianity, there is no doubt that the belief that we have the power within ourselves to create our futures has existed for a very long time.

In fact, one of Buddha's most significant teachings was, "What you have become is what you have thought," which underpins the intrinsic concept in the Law of Attraction. We are all familiar with the term "karma," a concept that permeates numerous spiritual and religious teachings. But no matter how it is framed, the idea is that whatever we put out into the world will return to us, be it good or bad, love or hate, happiness or anger.

This simple concept has been popular and widespread in our civilization, spanning many centuries, religions, and cultures. In Christianity, we read in Proverbs 23:7 that, "As a man thinketh in his heart so is he." It is evident that the Law of Attraction, in its many different iterations, has always existed and will always be there for anyone who wishes to explore its possibilities.

New Thought Traditions in the 19th Century

It wasn't until Madame Helena Blavatsky used the phrase "Law of Attraction" in her work that the term came into use. In the 19th century, a group of authors, religious groups, philosophers, and others came together with their shared belief that "God" and the "Universe" exist within all objects, places, and people. Together they explored the concepts of life force, visualization, metaphysics, positive thinking, and the Law of Attraction. Although many people were part of this movement, Helena Blavatsky and Thomas Troward were the most significant members.

Blavatsky traveled across many different countries, giving spiritual guidance and instruction, gaining a reputation of being incredibly gifted. Her book, *The Secret Doctrine*, used many traditions and concepts from ancient religions. Much of her teachings overlapped with what we now call and understand as the Law of Attraction. Most importantly, she introduced the idea that our thoughts about how we view ourselves and our identity define what it is we are capable of and who we inherently are. She affirmed that we have the power to change and shape our reality and to progress past our own perceived limitations. These key messages form part of modern teachings of manifestation. Or, as Blavatsky puts it, "The Universe is worked and guided from within outwards."

The Law of Attraction in the 20th and 21st Century

The Law of Attraction gained influence and popularity around the mid-20th century. Author Esther Hicks wrote a collection of nine books, called *The Teachings of Abraham*, in which she explained how the Law of Attraction works. She also included how manifestation through the Law of Attraction could be used to attain our desires.

At the same time, Louise Hay, another "New Thought" author, started to explore how affirmations can help us achieve our goals using the Law of Attraction. A firm believer in self-awareness, compassion, and love for oneself, she helped shape the belief that if you have a positive self-image, it can increase your vibrations and ultimately positively affect your capacity to manifest.

The 21st century hailed Rhonda Byrne and her book, *The Secret*, for bringing the niche concept of the Law of Attraction into the limelight of the modern era, with advice on how to apply it practically in our everyday life. A film based on the book included the teachings and views of several modern-day practitioners of the Law of Attraction, including Jack Canfield, Joe Vitale, and Marie Diamond. The film was quite popular because it made the concepts easy to understand and empowered individuals with its approach to manifestation. For example, it emphasizes how changing the way we think, set goals, and view our life negatively or positively are key to attaining our goals. It brought the Law of Attraction into the mainstream by making it accessible to anyone who wanted to use it, not just those who are experts or spiritually-inclined.

THE SCIENCE BEHIND THE LAW OF ATTRACTION

Within the 12 Universal Laws are the 7 Natural Laws. You are probably familiar with the Laws of Relativity and Cause and Effect, both proven and based in science, as are the Laws of Gender, Rhythm, and Polarity, which you see around you every day in nature in male and female species, the rising and setting of the sun, the motion of the tides, and the concept of everything having an opposite, like hot and cold. The other two Natural Laws are the Law of Attraction and the Law of Perpetual Transmutation of Energy.

The Law of Perpetual Transmutation

The Law of Perpetual Transmutation explains that in the universe, everything that we can touch, hear, smell, taste, or see, as well as our emotions, are all made up of energy moving in various states of vibration. This energy is perpetual, meaning it can't be destroyed or created, only transferred or changed in constant motion. The Law of Perpetual Transmutation tells us that this nonphysical energy is constantly evolving into a physical state.

Our thoughts are made of this energy, so any image or idea that we think about and give consciousness to must change into its physical state. We express emotions through our body, which then responds accordingly. An example would be when you feel sad and then listen to a sad song, which makes you cry. The act of crying and your tears are a physical expression of your sadness and the energy it contains.

The Law of Vibration

The Law of Vibration is one of the 12 Universal Laws and explains that everything is always moving or vibrating and nothing is still. This vibration of energy is in everything around you, from the cells in your body to the tallest trees and buildings surrounding you. Everything vibrates at a specific frequency, including our emotions.

All of the thoughts we hold onto and to which we attach an emotion control our individual state of vibration. Once you become aware of this vibration, it becomes what you know to be your emotions. In turn, your feelings lead to the actions you take and the decisions you make, and ultimately influence your life experiences. Your feelings are directly connected to the results in your life because of what you are attracting.

According to the Law of Vibration, things with the same vibrational frequency are naturally drawn to each other. Consider the example of raindrops on a windowpane. As they run down the window, some of those droplets are attracted to each other and join together to form one larger droplet. This happens because they are vibrating at the same frequency. This same outcome won't happen if you try to join a droplet of oil with a droplet of water because they each have different vibrations.

The Law of Attraction

By understanding the Law of Attraction and how it works, you can shift your focus from allowing outside influences to control how you feel and think to be more inwardly focused and consciously choose the thoughts and feelings that correlate with what you want in your life. By actively taking control of your influences, you set the vibration and frequency to attract your desired results.

Consider these three key concepts:

- Everything has a vibration.
- Things that have similar vibrational frequencies are drawn to each other.
- You are capable of controlling and changing your vibration.

Together these three concepts work to help you control and create the outcomes you want in your life.

A fundamental flaw in how many people try to use the Law of Attraction is that they try to control and create what they want to happen without changing their vibration to align with their desired outcome. Remember that setting your vibrational frequency comes from inside and extends outward into a physical expression of your feelings. If your frequency is not aligned with your actions and what you want to attract, you are unlikely to achieve the desired results by simply willing them into being. However, if you deliberately adjust and control your internal vibration frequencies, you can set your vibration to your desired state.

Ultimately, you control your thoughts and feelings regarding your vibrational frequency. The Law of Attraction works by deliberately aligning your frequency with the outcomes you want to attract.

7 MYTHS AND MISCONCEPTIONS OF LOA

Before we go any further, we need to clear up some rumors and misconceptions about the Law of Attraction. You may have encountered these beliefs in warnings from others. Perhaps you even share some of them. For LOA to manifest what you want, you must whole-heartedly buy in to the idea. Any half-measures will influence your vibrational frequencies in ways not aligned with the things you want.

Avoid believing the following half-truths and falsehoods:

1 - LOA Is Magical!

Try this. Imagine what you want. Make a positive statement about it. See yourself owning your dream in reality. Now, do not waste another minute worrying about achieving your goal. What happened? Most likely—absolutely nothing.

You cannot "say a magic word, and your dream will be realized." That's smoke and mirrors. Your best possible existence will not be magically handed to you with no effort on your part. There is no stage magician using trap doors and other props to create a reality that isn't there. You will not be handed your dream existence on a silver platter because of some supernatural manifestation. Thinking alone without some form of action will simply be not enough.

The Law of Attraction is a natural process. It is in effect right now in your life, attracting the things to you that vibrate at your same energy level and frequency.

Sure, when you begin visualizing, using affirmations, meditating, and going through the manifestation process I will share with you in a bit, it may seem magical when you start to receive the things you want. However, there is no magic involved. Magic does not exist. The Law of Attraction does. Nevertheless, it's up to you how you harness such energy. You are responsible for sending things in the right direction to realize the physical, emotional, financial, and spiritual rewards you are looking for.

2 - Science Can't Prove the Law of Attraction

We've already discussed several instances in which science has proven that the Law of Attraction exists in the natural world, and there is other research that supports the idea that you are constantly attracting energy.

Think about it this way...

The propane or natural gas that powers products in our homes is invisible. Natural gas does not have a smell, so a detectable odor is added to it so we will know when we have a gas leak. Just because you cannot see this gas and, in some cases, cannot even smell it, does not mean it cannot kill you.

The Law of Attraction works the same way.

Just because you cannot see the vibrational energy that all things give off does not mean it isn't there. You do not need to understand the Law of Attraction or be able to touch, feel, or see it for it to work. Electricity is invisible, but if you were to stick your finger in a light socket, it would let you know it is there. LOA has been scientifically proven, which means your belief in this powerful, natural law can grow stronger because you know it exists. With this information in mind, we can learn to harness it.

3 - LOA Doesn't Work

This is one of the biggest myths you will hear about the Law of Attraction. Because it's invisible, many people do not believe it works. Those same people breathe invisible, odorless, and tasteless oxygen that keeps them alive every day, but they will tell you that since they can't see, smell, or hear LOA, it can't be real.

If it does not exist in their eyes, how can it work?

When you begin embracing the Law of Attraction, thinking positively, and keeping your vibrations high, you will start to see LOA working in your life. When you consistently work through the five steps needed to manifest what you want (don't worry, we'll get to this later), you will have no doubt that like energies attract each other.

Just as gravity existed long before Newton explained it, so too has the LOA been around forever. As long as the natural world has been in existence, similar energy frequencies have been in play.

4 - LOA Requires Too Much Effort

Some people will tell you the Law of Attraction is hard to get a grip on and therefore not worth the effort to pursue. But it's not hard and it does all the work. All you have to do is get your energy right. If you are just learning to use the Law of Attraction to push your desires toward you, there will be some work involved in learning how to control your thoughts. But soon enough, the process begins to work on its own. You learn to act and think in a way that focuses your energy and intent so that the things you desire are magnetized and pulled toward you.

If you think LOA requires too much effort, consider your present reality. How long have you been banging your head against the wall to try to get what you desire? How many years or decades have you lived a life that is a watered-down version of what you know you deserve? You have probably spent countless tireless hours trying to create your dream reality, yet you are still not where you want to be. A poor and negative mindset is restrictive and evident in many people's lives. Such thoughts are nothing more than excuses brought about by self-limiting beliefs.

5 - The Law of Attraction Is Based on Self-Centered and Greedy Desires

Some people believe the pursuit of money is evil. They may tell you that the Bible says, "Money is the root of all evil." In fact, the Bible says, "The *love* of money is the root of all evil."

Wanting money is not a bad thing. Enjoying abundance in any form is not bad either. What you do with the abundance that the Law of Attraction delivers to you is up to you. You can certainly use your newfound wealth, health, intelligence, influence, or possessions to do bad things. That is your choice. However, what you will find with the Law of Attraction is that when you begin to act in a negative manner in the eyes of the universe, all you will attract is negative energy.

On the contrary, the Law of Attraction is not based on helping greedy and self-centered people. Those are negative emotions and energies. They will only attract negative results and outcomes. Besides, is it self-centered and greedy to want a fulfilled, happy, and rewarding life? Is it wrong that you want to finally live in harmony with the person you were intended to be? Of course not. The people who suggest that LOA is for greedy, self-centered people either do not know what they're talking about, or they do not want to see you succeed.

6 - You Can't Practice LOA If You Have Certain Religious Beliefs

I'll say it again. The Law of Attraction is natural. There is no witchcraft or voodoo involved.

It is not a supernatural or magical undertaking. LOA does not care whether you practice a specific religion, or if you consider yourself a spiritual being of some type. You are a natural being because you are a product of nature, so when LOA detects your energy and attracts similar energies to you, it is doing so in accordance with the natural order of things.

Would your religion tell you that the stars in the heavens, the trees and the mountains, the oceans and the deserts are all off-limits? Surely, they would not. They tell you that these are beautiful things created by nature, and are gifts we should all appreciate. The Law of Attraction is also a natural gift, and is already working in your life, so it only makes sense to make sure it works for you rather than against you.

Incidentally, when you start living a life of harmony with the universe, your appreciation of your spirituality or religion can only become more powerful.

7 - Law of Attraction Is Not for Everyone

The Law of Attraction is objective. It does not have an opinion about you or anyone else. It does not have anything to say about rocks or trees or cars or money or wealth or health or the 20 pounds you want to lose.

It works for everyone and everything that gives off energy, automatically and without judgment.

It is as natural and uncaring as fire. If you burn your hand on a flame, it is not because the fire does not like you. Anyone who walks up to a fire and sticks their hand in it will have the same experience—LOA works the same way.

HOW THE LAW OF ATTRACTION WORKS

If the Law of Attraction seems simple, you might wonder why so few people use it to succeed and be happy in life. But there's more to it than just knowing that the law exists. You first have to understand the workings of it before putting it to good use.

There are two approaches to explaining how this concept works for your benefit—spiritual and scientific. Understanding both will help you find what is best suited to your current situation or what you might be more comfortable with. For example, if you believe that you can attract good things to your life by aligning your desires with the plans God has for you, you might choose to use the spiritual approach.

On the other hand, the scientific approach may be better suited for you by using positive thinking, allowing you to take more risks, be open to new opportunities, and embrace new possibilities. But, if you let negative thoughts prevail, there will surely be missed opportunities, because you believe that you do not deserve them.

The Spiritual Explanation

The Law of Attraction works if you align your wishes with what God has in store for you. The human body can be thought of as an "energy field," making you and everyone else a "spiritual being." Just like all forms of energy, we all vibrate at a particular frequency. Our thoughts and feelings determine this frequency, and all the things we desire also have energy vibrating at a specific frequency.

When you start thinking about what you want, you release that frequency and cause the energy of the object you desire to vibrate at the same frequency. This is how you bring that object to you. The more you focus on what you want, the more you change its vibration until it reaches your frequency and is drawn to you.

Thoughts are magnetic and have a frequency of their own. When you send those thoughts out into the world, they magnetically draw the things existing on the same frequency. This makes you a human transmission tower. You transmit through your thoughts and receive pictures of those thoughts in the form of the things and events in your life.

Your ability to transmit your thoughts and realize them attracts the good while avoiding the bad. Stop thinking about what you do not want and focus more on what you *do* want. The law cannot distinguish good from bad thoughts, so if you keep thinking about your long list of debt, you are emitting that negative thought to the universe. You are affirming it, so that is what you will draw to you. Instead, think about how you will pay off those debts, and continue to think these kinds of thoughts until positive things and opportunities show themselves to you.

Remember that the Law of Attraction does not care what the feelings are behind your thoughts. It merely responds to your vibration. If you start interpreting a situation as "bad," you tend to experience other bad things, or even worse ones. To avoid this, make a conscious effort to think positively, no matter how dire your situation. Seek that silver lining to avoid attracting a series of negative things.

Think about when you wake up in the morning and start off on the wrong foot. You forget your keys to your office at home, and start thinking of this as something terrible, then you get stuck in traffic while returning home to retrieve them. When you finally arrive at the office, you find you've missed a meeting with an important client who has just barely been persuaded to reschedule another meeting with you. This situation took a turn for the worse because you chose to activate the magnet that attracted the wrong things.

Achieving what you desire starts with acknowledging the existence of an Intelligent Substance, from where all things come. This should be followed by believing that the Substance will reward you with what you desire. You can continue getting what you wish by expressing profound gratitude toward this Substance, often referred to as God.

For the Law of Attraction to work, you should cultivate the habit of showing gratitude for every good thing you are blessed with. To avoid attracting negativity to your life, do not let your mind wander onto the wrong things. Instead, focus on the good things still in transmission toward you.

The Traditional Scientific Explanation

The Law of Attraction can also be explained using the scientific approach. Several studies in neuroscience, evolutionary biology, and psychology can help you better understand how this law works. Most of this research focuses on how positive thinking also helps people attract positive things to their lives, which is essentially what the Law of Attraction is all about.

One Korean study, in fact, found that positive thinking helps predict a person's ability to experience life satisfaction. Optimism and life satisfaction also differ significantly in groups showing diverse demographic variables. This study showed that Koreans in their 20s and 30s rated themselves higher than older people in terms of optimism and life satisfaction. People who had higher education or finished college and those who were wealthier also scored higher in the same factors. But the study also found that demographic factors alone do not determine people's happiness.

People who scored high on positive thinking also scored high on life satisfaction. This showed that positive thinking could help improve life satisfaction. One of the findings stated that introducing psychological interventions such as optimism could be an effective approach to promoting life satisfaction.

Another study examined longitudinal, cross-sectional, and experimental data. It showed that positive emotions and lasting happiness are usually associated with characteristics linked to a successful and thriving life. These characteristics include optimism, sociability, originality, energy, and altruism.

In the study, happiness is defined as the frequent presence of positive emotions. The researchers concluded that happiness leads to success. Happy people are more likely to enjoy fulfilling relationships, excellent work performances, high incomes, good health, more active community involvement, and long life. As the Law of Attraction states, being positive attracts positive things and circumstances to your life.

An excellent example of how this might play out in real life would be how having a positive disposition can lead to people liking you and feeling comfortable with you faster than they might with someone else. And if you attend a business meeting emitting that positive aura, you might have a higher chance of closing that deal because of the confidence you exude.

Another example might be how happy employees often receive positive evaluations from their supervisors, have higher productivity, and deal more effectively with managerial tasks. They also tend to have a lower risk of burning out or exhibiting counterproductive workplace behavior. The same success story goes for happy people in various aspects of their lives—friendships, marriage, income, and health.

A positive-thinking study showed the power of positive visualization on respondents diagnosed with general anxiety disorder. One group visualized positive outcomes for three of their more recent worries, another thought of positive verbal results, and the third group visualized positive images whenever their fears started creeping in.

The two groups that thought of positive visual images, whether related to their worries or not, reported increased restfulness, greater happiness, and reduced anxiety. Practicing positive ideation helped the participants reduce the occurrence of more worry-related thoughts, though not the level of negativity of these thoughts. The findings suggested that it helps to disengage from such thoughts and focus instead on more positive images in your head.

All these studies showed that we draw positive things to our lives when we start thinking positively. The Law of Attraction does work, and it works well.

2

THE REAL REASON IT HASN'T WORKED FOR YOU YET

Imagine you're learning about the Law of Attraction for the very first time, and someone tells you that you can use it to unlock every desire you've ever had in your life.

You're even given a wonderfully easy 'technique' or 'method' to attract these things. You're then told all you have to do is the straightforward work of running through your 'process' every day, and then everything you want will come to you. Pretty easy, right?

Well, if all of this is true and the methods for achieving this really are as easy as you've been told, then why does manifesting your desires always feel so impossible? Why is it so tough to follow through and do the techniques every day? Why, when you actually manage to do them, don't they seem to work? And why does it feel like no matter how hard you try, how much you do, or how many techniques you use, nothing ever seems to happen for you? The answer is your ego.

When I say "ego," I'm not talking about it in the "overconfident" or "arrogant" sense of the word. I'm talking about the part of your consciousness in which your true identity is rooted. The part of your mind that you use to cope with your surroundings and maintain stability in your life.

You see, even with everything the universe can do for you, you're still operating on a plane of existence where your beliefs and mindset affect how much you allow into your life. This means your solution needs to include both an understanding of your psychology AND an approach for how to use that psychology to your advantage (rather than letting it hold you back).

So, what exactly is the ego? It's the part of your mind that lies between your conscious and subconscious.

3 MINDS: THE CONSCIOUS, THE SUBCONSCIOUS, AND THE EGO

Your conscious mind is everything you're aware (and in control) of. It's the source of your willpower.

Your subconscious mind is just about everything else. And it's exponentially more powerful than any other part of your mind (including the ego). Once your subconscious has determined or accepted something as "real," it will bring it into your life, whether you like it or not.

For example, let's say you want to make a million dollars, and you successfully convince your subconscious that this is now your reality. It will then act as a sort of supercomputer that runs on autopilot to move you into corresponding circumstances without you even realizing it.

You might find yourself coming up with amazing ideas, saying all the right things to all the right people, and making 'guesses' that end up being wildly successful. All because this supercomputer calculated every possible step needed to accomplish these things and then effortlessly executed the plan using your actions.

And yes, it IS that powerful!

But it goes deeper than simply controlling your actions. Since it doesn't have the same hangups or insecurities that your conscious mind might have, your subconscious is more intimately connected to the rest of the universal mind, so it can send signals to other people who can help you accomplish your goals.

For example, it might subconsciously instruct the manager at the bank to give you a loan, even if you're not qualified. Or it may guide that casting director to view your audition tape AND like it (even if they don't understand why). Or it may do something else that you may not even be aware of to line up the opportunities you need to achieve your goal.

Sometimes you won't know precisely WHY or HOW this all works. But you don't need to know to enjoy the benefits. The point is, your ego is stronger than your conscious mind but not as powerful as your subconscious, which is why you haven't been able to use the Law of Attraction yet to manifest your desires.

You see, your ego is a survival mechanism. Its ONLY purpose is to make sure you stay alive. Your ego is hard-wired in, it's stubborn as hell, and it knows exactly what it's doing. And it can outlast your conscious willpower no matter how determined you think you are.

It's always going to be more powerful than any conscious impulse you have. And all it knows is that RIGHT NOW—at this moment—YOU ARE ALIVE. Even if nothing in your life -

your financial situation, your career, your level of happiness - is enjoyable, you're still currently surviving.

And there's no way for your ego to know that you'd remain alive if ANY of these conditions changed. THAT'S the problem. Your ego is desperately afraid of change because ANY change, even one that's obviously positive to your conscious mind, is a threat to the status quo that could potentially result in you no longer being alive. That's how the ego perceives it.

More money isn't necessarily better for you. Not that the ego thinks a great deal about this, but for all it knows, becoming rich and famous could result in a psycho stalker coming after you and threatening your life.

Sure, being wealthy may be pleasant, but your ego is not interested in your happiness. It's not even interested in your comfort. All it cares about is your survival. And all it knows is that whatever you've been doing is working (including your habit of struggling to improve your life!). So it won't risk allowing any change to your state of being that might lower the odds of your safety.

The ego was very useful back when we lived in caves and had to hunt our meals. You'd see a tiger, and your ego that would override any impulse you may have had to walk over and pet it. It was your ego that made sure you knew when to run, when to hide, when to fight, and when to rest.

Want to know what your ego is thinking RIGHT NOW?

Probably something along the lines of: "I'm alive. I like being alive. I want to stay this way. I fear change. Change might kill me. I wouldn't like that. I stop change from happening in any way I can."

Now, even though it thinks of things on this very basic level, it's also extremely shrewd when it needs to be. It instinctively knows all of your conscious mind's weaknesses, and it's well-practiced in exploiting them to the point where you rarely even notice it happening. It knows how to use doubt, fear, insecurity, uncertainty, impatience, and confusion to keep you in your place. And it can be deceptively convincing when it needs to be.

Think about it... Why is it that you've probably already learned many techniques for attracting the life of your dreams, and yet you still haven't been able to use them?

What's wrong with these techniques? Are they not enjoyable? Too complicated? Too confusing? Too simple? Too good to be true? Too time-consuming? Too inconvenient to fit your lifestyle?

Do you find yourself saying, "I'll start using them tomorrow"?

Do you lose your patience when you're doing them?

Do they feel like a chore?

Do they seem unreliable?

Do you struggle to do them daily?

Do you do them daily but struggle to focus each time?

Do you doubt they're even working?

Do you get bored with them?

Have you started a technique in the past, actually made some progress, seen early results, and then STILL somehow failed to stick with it or ride the momentum to any of your REAL goals?

Does there always seem to be SOMETHING in the way?

Are you reading book after book because you need the "perfect" explanation for how all of this works before you can finally allow yourself to commit to it completely?

Does it all feel so... hopeless?

ALL OF THESE REACTIONS ARE YOUR EGO'S ATTEMPT TO KEEP YOU ALIVE.

Notice that you're not consciously in control of any of this. It all just "seems to happen." This is what you're up against. Your ego doesn't understand that the changes you're trying to make are safe. It doesn't get that some of these changes might even be better for your health and survival. And no matter how much you want it, your willpower will never be enough to overtake the ego's plan to keep you alive. Your survival is just too important.

It's like getting in the ring with a 600-pound grizzly bear. You're never going to overpower it.

In spite of all this, there's one thing you need to understand: Even though it's holding you back, your ego is not your enemy. In fact, your ego is one of your best friends. It loves you deeply, and thinks that it's protecting you by keeping you where you are. If you think about the massive effort it exerts to keep you safe, it's really quite miraculous. By viewing your ego as your friend rather than your enemy, you'll find the techniques in this book much more effective.

And once you start to manifest what you want and your ego sees how awesome your new level of success is, it will notice that you survived and will then fight tooth and nail on your behalf to keep you from back-sliding (after all, that would be another change, and we all know how the ego feels about change). This leaves us with only one question: how do we overcome the ego to do all of this?

Well, just as your conscious mind is no match for your ego, your ego is just as helpless against your subconscious mind. It doesn't matter what your ego tries; your subconscious is much too strong, unbeatable, unstoppable, and impossible to outlast or overwhelm. So all we need is an easy way to bypass the ego and set our desired point of attraction directly with our subconscious mind instead. Everything after that will take care of itself.

3

REPROGRAMMING YOUR SUBCONSCIOUS MIND FOR MANIFESTATION

The different experiences you encounter in life are not always sudden or caused by good or back luck. Your experiences are a manifestation of your thoughts and feelings, and your subconscious mind plays a significant role in that. Intrigued?

Your intrigue shows how unaware you are of your own power, a power locked inside you waiting for you to tap into it. A power so strong that it can beautifully transform your life, and a power that has been given to all of us, so we can live an empowered life.

Our subconscious mind possesses this power, and while many people believe it to be something that cannot be unleashed, it is, in fact, quite doable. But first we must understand how our mind functions.

THE CONSCIOUS, UNCONSCIOUS, AND SUBCONSCIOUS MINDS

It isn't easy to explicitly define the subconscious mind, as our conscious and subconscious minds are always working together and feel like one thing.

Your mind functions on three main levels. Your conscious mind is the state you actively use when you do anything with full awareness. It is what you put to use when actively participating in a conversation, cooking, driving, reading, or doing anything else with complete consciousness.

While your conscious mind is in charge of things you do with complete awareness, the truth is, we aren't always working with 100% consciousness. Our mind often functions on autopilot, and if you pay attention to how you carry out many of your tasks, you will realize that you often function mechanically.

For instance, when driving, we may automatically apply the brakes when we reach a red light. While we consciously see the traffic light turn red, our foot automatically hits the brake pedal without us consciously making that decision.

When you walk into your house, you may unconsciously remove your shoes at the door, change into house slippers and close the door. Maybe you then move to your bathroom or bedroom and put your clothes in the laundry hamper as you do every day. You are so accustomed to this routine that you may not consciously realize what tasks you engage in. Only when you go through the list with complete attention do you acknowledge what you have been doing.

While you engage in these tasks in the moment, your entire mind may not be present while doing them. This happens because your subconscious mind has allowed you to nurture habits and allows you to function on autopilot to save you time, energy, and effort.

Your conscious mind engages in activities based on the efforts of your unconscious and subconscious minds. Your unconscious mind stores all the information you have picked up over the years, including fears, things you have seen, smelled, touched and tasted, every interaction you have had, and everything in between.

Your unconscious mind is indeed a massive storehouse of information. To prevent information overload, your subconscious mind picks out the most important memories and information based on how emotionally involved you were in certain situations, how much you repeat certain activities and how much something means to you.

It stores recently formed memories and creates a program of how we should work based on all the information locked in our unconscious mind. If you were fond of balloons when you were young and have been regularly buying balloons ever since, that means your subconscious mind has caused you to nurture a fondness for balloons. If you have been drinking four glasses of water every day since you were 12, your subconscious mind picks up that information and uses it to create that habit.

Likewise, it chooses the beliefs, ideas, viewpoints, fears, inhibitions, doubts, and sentiments you have and uses them to build your program. If you have been smoking for a while and feel it helps you cope with stress, your subconscious will make you nurture that belief.

Even so, if you think you can overcome an addiction, you will have that belief, and you will have the willpower courtesy of that belief, as well as the program created by your subconscious mind based on this belief.

Throughout the day, your subconscious collects data and sorts through it to figure out if you might need it at any time in the future. It stores information for a while, but if you don't come back looking for it, it tosses it out to the unconscious mind. Every piece of information you have ever picked up is in your unconscious mind, and if you wish to dig it out, you can do so by putting your subconscious mind to use.

The Power of the Subconscious Mind

To succeed in life, do what you aspire to do, manifest all your ambitions, and push yourself to do your best, you need to harness the power of the subconscious mind.

While you cannot control all the external factors and events you encounter, you can definitely control and manage your thoughts and perceptions. This perception can help us turn even the most unfavorable events in our favor.

As we discussed, the subconscious builds our internal program, which makes us react and respond to different things in different ways. It picks up from our unconscious mind that we have mostly chickened out of doing things that seem tough. It makes us nurture the belief that we cannot overcome our fears.

It is important to point out that our thoughts travel out into the universe and draw toward them other ideas vibrating on a similar frequency. Remember that everything in the universe is composed of energy and has a specific vibration that it exudes at all times. Things that share a similar vibration are drawn toward one another, which is why we have the saying, "like attracts like."

Yes, even humans exude energy and vibration through our thoughts, emotions, and feelings. These feelings and thoughts travel out into the universe and interact with other thoughts and emotions and those that vibrate at a similar frequency mingle and are drawn toward each other.

Every thought is accompanied by a host of events, experiences, ideas, concepts, and people associated with it. Hence, when a couple of thoughts interact, they bring with them all these related elements.

When you come across someone in a social situation who is as passionate as you are about plants and is a staunch environmentalist like you, it is because your thoughts and those of that person met somewhere in the universe and made a connection of their own. They then bring you and the other person together because the two of you share the same energy and vibration.

Similarly, everything that you feel drawn toward you happens because of the thoughts brewed up by your subconscious. Your thoughts bring all the good and the not-so-good experiences closer to you.

If you keep thinking that bad things will happen to you, eventually, you will face bad things. Remember when you worried about how terrible your job interview would go, and you ended up making a fool of yourself? What about when you were confident your mortgage would be approved, and even though your credit history was not ideal, you knew it would work out.

Think of other similar events when you were and were not so positive about certain outcomes. You might be surprised to learn that your confidence and inhibitions caused you to experience outcomes according to your expectations.

All of this occurs because of your subconscious mind. If you wish to change outcomes and experiences, you only need to reprogram this wonderful tool.

You Can Control the Power of Your Subconscious

Your subconscious mind is a tricky creature. It receives information without question. Whatever you tell it must be true, which means that reprogramming it should be straightforward, right?

In theory, yes. The problem is that most of us have picked up stories and assimilated them so successfully that we aren't even aware they're there. Whether it was a parent or loved one putting us down, or whether we simply decided for ourselves that nothing good ever happens to us, there will be thought patterns hardwired into our mind that we need to remove before we can experience the kind of success we all deserve.

Luckily, this doesn't have to be a complicated, drawn-out process.

A thought pattern is an established habit of thinking in a particular manner. It is usually so ingrained that you aren't even aware of it, and it's that lack of awareness that makes it so hard to identify.

Human beings are creatures of habit. The more frequently we do something, the more likely it is we'll do it again in the future, even if it's reinforcing negative consequences. So, you might recognize on a surface level that shouting at your partner when you come home after a tough day at work isn't helping your relationship. It can be challenging to try a different approach. If you don't see immediate results, it's easy to slide back into bad habits because you've 'tried everything else.' You probably haven't, or if you have tried another way, you probably haven't given it long enough. Still, repetition creates neural pathways in the brain that reassure us of familiarity, and our egos love familiarity! Familiarity is safe. Familiarity means that everything will stay the same and reinforce the reality we live in, and that's great if you love your life, but not so much if you don't.

Although we love to think that we've evolved as a species, underneath it all, we're still living back in the days where danger lurked around every corner and hunters might not survive the food search. So, when we have thought patterns that give us a predictable response, our ego says, "Great! We're safe for another day! Let's keep doing that!"

This is why we choose a miserable life over an abundant one. It's safe.

This is why the thought of success is so terrifying. It's new. It's different. It's unpredictable. We have no idea whether what we want will work out for us. It's less frightening to stay where we are, even though we're not happy.

If you find your ego sending you warning signals every time you think about doing things differently, thank it. It's only doing its job, after all. Say, "Thank you for keeping me safe, but I'm going to try a new way." You may be surprised at how acknowledging your ego's concerns goes a long way toward keeping those concerns in context. You are not going to create a new, abundant life by doing things the way you always have, so you will have to change—and your ego will have to be okay with that.

Every thought generates a chemical reaction in the brain, which then provokes an emotional response. As you give this thought attention, it builds a new circuit that sends complex signals to the body, shaping your reality. The more you repeat this cycle, the more entrenched the thought becomes, developing a habit.

So, if you've been attracting one cheating boyfriend after another or bouncing from one dead-end job to another in the mistaken belief that you're making progress in your career, now you know why.

Our subconscious mind is continually working, running an incredible 95% of our life without conscious thought. Neuroscience research has discovered that most of our decisions, behaviors, and emotions are driven by subconscious brain activity. The way our subconscious mind is programmed dictates 95% of our life and affects the remaining 5%.

This programming starts from the moment we take our first breath, so you may not even remember the early experiences that generated some of your self-destructive thought patterns.

A friend of mine has two beautiful daughters. They're equally stunning, and both have been brought up with supportive parents who have done everything they can to give the girls healthy self-esteem. Yet while one of them has complete confidence in her appearance, the other is convinced she's unattractive, and nothing anyone can say will persuade her otherwise.

The only explanation my friend can come up with for why this is dates back to when the girls were babies. The older girl was a beautiful baby and always had people telling her how gorgeous she was. The other was a very hairy baby. Still adorable, but strangers weren't anywhere as complimentary. Some of them could be downright rude, calling her names.

Your subconscious mind is insidious and contains thought patterns programmed from memories you can't actively recall. Those thought patterns have been repeated so often that it is difficult to separate yourself from them. Once you have decided that something is true about yourself, it is hard to shift that belief, especially since your mind will actively look for evidence supporting that belief and ignore anything that counters it.

If you have decided that you're a loser, every time you make a mistake, you'll take it as proof that you're a loser. Every time you succeed (which may well be more often than you realize), you'll discount it as a lucky one-off. That cycle will continue until you remove that programming.

You can view these thought patterns as stories. They are stories you tell yourself and believe to be true. As famed psychoanalyst Carl Jung put it, "Until you make the unconscious conscious, it will direct your life, and you will call it fate." The good news is that these stories are just fiction, and fiction can be rewritten!

Rewrite your stories, and you will genuinely rewrite reality.

Controlling the stories in your mind is an ongoing process. It requires a lifetime commitment to noticing when unwanted patterns creep in. Fortunately, as human beings, we have something called 'neuroplasticity.' This is the ability to rewire our brain to create new thought patterns and behavior. We have limitless potential for our brain cells to fire and wire together in new, exciting ways.

You are not the product of your thoughts; you are the product of the thoughts you choose to empower. You are always in control of this process. The question is whether you've made the active decision to control it or whether you're letting your subconscious mind take the wheel.

Your mind is constantly generating thoughts. These thoughts are of no consequence until you decide to give them attention. You choose to nurture the positive or negative, and whatever choice you make will deliver results. It's neuroscience!

The process of developing new thought patterns is straightforward, but that doesn't mean it's not hard work. It requires a level of self-awareness you may not think is possible and involves something called 'metacognition,' which means actively thinking about your thinking.

There are three steps to follow:

1. Observe your current emotional and physical state.
2. Pay more attention to which thoughts you entertain.
3. Repeat steps 1 and 2.

Mindfulness is popular because it helps ground you in the moment, free from worry and stress about the future. You can use mindfulness exercises to support you in this process.

For example, you can set a regular alarm to check in with your current state, perhaps once an hour. When it goes off, close your eyes and ask yourself, "What am I thinking? How am I feeling?" Observe your thoughts and emotions without judgment. Simply be aware of what is currently going on in your mind. You might like to journal these thoughts and emotions to find any recurring ideas and feelings that could suggest a pattern you need to rewire. This is a very effective exercise, especially if you are new to the practice of controlling your mind.

Another exercise involves pausing when you feel overwhelmed by a particular emotion, whether good or bad. Ask yourself, "What am I thinking? How am I feeling? What thought has made me feel this way?"

Again, you might find it helpful to journal your observations to help you figure out the story you've been telling yourself that made you feel this way. If you haven't got time to stop and actually write something out, you can use a recording app on your phone to vocalize what's going on at that moment. Maybe you don't know, and that's okay. The simple process of actively choosing to be more conscious with your thinking will help you become more self-aware in a brief period.

Once you have identified the negative thought patterns that automatically drive your behavior, you can begin rewriting them.

Make a list of the stories that are no longer serving you. It might look something like this:

- I am always blamed for everything.
- No one ever listens to me.
- I always have bad luck.
- Nobody likes me.

Now rewrite those stories to create a more positive reality:

- I am not responsible for other people's opinions.
- I am an effective communicator.
- I create my own good luck.
- I am worthy of being liked.

Every time you find yourself following an old story, stop and tell yourself your new story and consciously observe how it changes your mood and thought patterns. If you can, look at yourself in the mirror while you repeat your affirmation—looking yourself in the eye helps this process. Even if that is not practical, this exercise will still be effective.

If you're struggling to believe your new stories, that's okay. It takes a while to completely remove that old hardwiring. However, if you can, do something to reinforce your new story. For example, if you think nobody likes you, chances are you know people who like you but you have discounted those relationships because they don't match your story. Tell yourself, "I am worthy of being liked," and send someone you know and like a quick text or private message on social media to let them know you're thinking about them.

And if you genuinely cannot think of a single person who likes you, then take steps to rectify that! Join social media groups with like-minded people. Push yourself out of your comfort zone and try a new activity. Reach out to someone you've always wanted to get to know better but haven't made an effort. You might experience a few setbacks because of your old programming, but focus on your new story and know that you really are worthy of being liked.

The more you start thinking in a way that aligns with the reality you want to manifest, the faster that reality will appear because you will have raised your vibration to its level and naturally attract people and experiences that match that vibe.

10 TECHNIQUES TO BECOME A MASTER OF YOUR SUBCONSCIOUS MIND

In this section, you'll find ten techniques to begin consciously mastering your mind power. It may be that you are aware of, or even practice, many of these. Those who are well-informed in Law of Attraction principles undoubtedly will understand the basics, such as visualization, affirmations, and meditation. However, many of you might find it valuable to study these tips and the information provided to solidify your knowledge and understand the reasoning and importance of executing these actions in a precise manner.

1: Risk-Taking

Superior men and women are constantly pushing themselves to go beyond their comfort zones. They understand how fast a person's comfort zone can become a rut. They realize that complacency is the sworn enemy of innovation and future potential. Because the subconscious mind perceives unknowns as frightening, the risk becomes an essential aspect of success, and overriding those fears allows change.

Allowing for an unknown variable—anything other than what the mind is already aware of—is required to produce a change in your subconscious patterns. The mind believes it has all the answers. In certain ways, it does. It may even be aware of all possibilities, but it must believe in each one individually.

You must challenge your subconscious mind by forcing it to search out fresh factors if you want a new life. Allow yourself to feel awkward and uncomfortable the first few times you try something new. When you try to disrupt any of your established behavior patterns, your subconscious mind makes you feel emotionally and physically uncomfortable. On the other hand, risk-taking tests the limits and generates expanded comfort zones in the subconscious mind.

There is a widespread belief that taking chances is dangerous. To be honest, taking risks is no more dangerous than playing it safe or sticking to the status quo. In fact, by failing to innovate, alter, and progress in all aspects of our lives, we expose ourselves to the risk of stagnation and falling behind. Without taking risks, the likelihood of expanding beyond what was previously known is greatly reduced. When it comes to risk, new causes set in action new effects.

Of course, there's always the chance of making mistakes or failing to achieve the desired objectives. The world's most successful people recognize that failure is what drives them to attain their dreams. It's their attitude toward so-called failure that sets them apart from everyone else. They don't mind failing since they can see the benefits of their efforts. If one risk does not work out, they investigate a new risk rather than accepting irreversible failure; as a result, their subconscious patterning is altered.

With this type of behavior and attitude, the subconscious mind has no choice but to accept that the conscious mind has made a firm decision to keep trying until it succeeds. Once this form of surrender occurs within the subconscious, existing restrictions are replaced with grander standards that attract new outcomes.

#2: **Auto-Inquisition**

Auto-inquisition is the name given to a process that can be formatted in any way that works best for you. It was utilized by musicians like Beethoven and Bach, and inventors like Thomas Edison. Edison would nap in his favorite chair while holding a metal ball in each hand. He would concentrate on a question about a topic he was working on. As he began to nod off, his palms would loosen and the balls would fall to the floor, jolting him awake. This allowed him to remain in the twilight state between sleeping and dreaming, where he could access the information stored in his subconscious mind. He felt this was when he was most creative. When combined with auto-inquisition, this drowsy state is a perfect creative playground, capable of manifesting solutions with astounding results.

Asking questions right before bedtime, when you're comfortable and about to go asleep, will improve your auto-inquisition success rate. After falling asleep with a query in mind, many people awaken to find that the answer to the next step toward their objective has mysteriously been supplied.

Asking the subconscious mind questions is a solid technique to influence it. Questions allow for unknown variables and open the mind to new possibilities. The subconscious is programmed to assist you in finding an answer or solving a problem you're having trouble with by taking the most direct route to the answer. It follows the path of least resistance and works on the principle of least effort. Once again, this is for your own safety.

Is it possible to dismiss a query? Is it possible to dismiss this? It's worth noting that your subconscious mind answered each of those questions before you even consciously thought of responding. A question cannot be ignored; it must be processed into a response before the brain even recognizes the question. We can take advantage of this.

To get past the subconscious mind's barriers, the trick is to phrase the queries in a specific way. "What else is feasible that I haven't considered?" is an example of a query that allows for this. When faced with a question like this, the subconscious mind is forced to look for something new because it has already explored all known possibilities. It will keep looking for the answer until it finds it.

When you ask your subconscious questions about your desires, it is prompted to seek answers right away. "How awesome is it that I have so much money?" is one example. "How am I going to spend all of this money? How do I get ahead in life? How can I make this happen?" These are questions that your subconscious mind can't ignore. It processes and tries to respond to questions as soon as possible. Your brain has already answered the question, and your subconscious holds the answer for you.

"What-if" style inquiries also appeal to the subconscious mind. "What if I achieved my objectives?" "What would that look like?" you wonder. We may affect more change in our lives if we continue to ask questions and seek out new ones. The mind comes to conclusions that allow for continued progress because it subconsciously seeks answers. Continually challenging your subconscious mind with "What else is conceivable?" and "What if" questions will keep it on its metaphorical toes and help you achieve your goals.

#3: Empowering Thoughts and Precision Affirmations

Keep in mind that your subconscious mind is always listening to your conscious thoughts and conversations you have with yourself and others. As a result, choose thoughts and affirmations that empower you. Your brain will implant positive, precise affirmations about your intelligence and skills into new neural pathways and produce the desired effects if you believe them sincerely.

Knowing what's going on inside your conscious mind is the most effective way to tap into the limitless power of your subconscious mind. Few of us pay attention to what we're thinking about during the day, allowing random thoughts to float around in our heads. But successful people have a great deal of control over their thinking. When you consciously choose and control your ideas, you can use the Law of Attraction to your advantage within your subconscious mind.

Words, sentences, mental images, and sensations are used in thinking. Thoughts are visitors who come to the mind's central station. They arise, stay for a short time, and then vanish, leaving room for new ideas. Some of these thoughts linger longer, gather force, and have an impact on the lives of those who think them. It's critical to pay attention to what goes into the subconscious mind. Words and repeated thoughts gain strength over time, sink into the subconscious, and influence behavior, actions, reactions, and external events and circumstances.

The subconscious mind interprets the words and concepts that become lodged inside it as expressing and characterizing an actual situation, and hence tries to align these words and concepts with reality. It works tirelessly to bring them to life in the lives of those who say or think them. Your life will begin to alter if you consciously choose the thoughts, phrases, and words you repeat in your mind. Through the power of affirmations, you will start to create new conditions and circumstances.

Affirmations are statements that are repeated several times during the day, which sink into the subconscious mind and release its immense ability to manifest the intent of the words and phrases in the outside world. This isn't to suggest that every word you utter will have an effect. The words must be spoken with attention, intention, and feeling in order to activate the subconscious mind.

Affirmations must be expressed positively to see positive benefits from this strategy. Negatives, such as the words 'don't' and 'not,' are difficult for the subconscious mind to process. What do you think of if I tell you not to think about a pink elephant? Most likely you think about a pink elephant. This is why it's so important to frame affirmations and everyday thoughts in a good way.

When your goals are sufficiently ingrained in your subconscious mind, they activate a whole new law, called the Law of Expectation. This is a set of new perspectives on what is genuinely feasible for you to achieve. The Law of Correspondence mentioned earlier, which states that what happens around us is a direct reflection of what's happening within us, is then activated, and as a result, your energy level skyrockets, and your creativity is significantly boosted.

#4: **Repetition**

One of the most important rules that the subconscious mind follows is that beliefs are formed and strengthened via repetition. Reading the belief, hearing it, visualizing it, or mentally affirming it are all examples of repetition. When combined with emotion and feeling, repetition is the cause for all subconscious transformation. Thoughts and affirmations must be repeated over and over again as a technique of building new auto-pilot habits to create new beliefs.

Do you recall learning to drive a car for the first time? Operating the vehicle in a way that ensures your safety and precision requires the highest concentration and purposeful action. You probably spent every waking moment thinking about how to drive more efficiently. However, driving a vehicle becomes automatic after enough practice and deliberate guidance. The subconscious brain takes control and says, "Now that I know what to do, you can relax." It eventually becomes a subconscious process in which your conscious mind lets go while your body transports you to your destination.

The subconscious mind handles all established behavior in this manner. You have the choice to change your behavior and beliefs if they are not conducive to the outcomes you desire. On the other hand, the subconscious mind must repeat this directive again and again until it becomes automatic. Furthermore, your body's cells can learn a variety of daily acts, allowing them to take over numerous functions that were previously performed by the intellect. They follow instructions from your subconscious mind to guarantee that they respond to demands according to beliefs. This portion of the brain ensures that your actions and physical body strictly follow your programming. Repetition can create new programming that can be used to replace outmoded ways of behaving.

Similar to how you build strength in your body by going to the gym regularly, you must devote the same amount of time and effort to your mental muscles if you wish to see long-term results. The outcomes must pass through the stages of conscious thought, habitual thought, and automatic subconscious comprehension. Every person is different, but repetition becomes habitual between the 60 and 90-day mark. Some people can change their instinctive behavior in as little as 30 days, while others may require up to 6 months or more. The idea is to be persistent until your new behavior becomes second nature.

#5: Auto-Suggestion

Auto-suggestion is a type of self-induced suggestion in which an individual's ideas, feelings, or actions are controlled by themselves. It takes positive affirmations to the next level. Affirmations have a broad structure, whereas auto-suggestion techniques are employed to confirm your unique human spirit by bypassing your thinking mind and awareness of your material body. It's essentially the quiet talk we have with ourselves about ourselves. When we speak to ourselves, we also talk to our subconscious mind.

Your subconscious is your illogical, irrational, non-analytical mind, whereas your conscious mind is your logical, rational, and analytical mind. Whether anything makes logical sense or not, your subconscious will believe it. It never doubts anything you tell it truthfully. Auto-suggestion is a powerful method for efficiently changing the subconscious mind to attract wishes by declaring what you want to be. This, too, necessitates consistent repetition.

You've probably been employing auto-suggestion strategies your entire life, whether you realize it or not. You've used auto-suggestion if you've ever told yourself that you're rich, poor, fat, thin, lucky, unlucky, or anything else. Put yourself in a fully relaxed condition to use this method most effectively to achieve the things you want. If you know of any self-hypnosis or meditation techniques that can help with this, use them. If not, close your eyes and count backward from twenty to one while following your breathing, in and out, for a few minutes.

Create "I AM" statements that reflect the new you in a good light. This expresses your recommendation in the present tense and the first person, placing you in the exact moment when it is made. Give the auto-suggestions your full attention, repeating them over and over. "I am abundant in all areas of life," "I am a magnet for wonderful situations," or "I am the luckiest person I know" are some examples.

When these self-affirmations are repeated often enough, they ultimately sink into the subconscious mind and are accepted at face value. Positive phrases and statements about your nature have the power to influence your inner world, establish new beliefs, change vibrations, and eventually alter your reality. New brain waves begin to emerge, and your brain's functional structure undergoes a lasting transformation. Neuroscientists have discovered, based on years of research, that new communication channels between neurons are established as we transfer new information to the brain. A new existence can then be shaped and manifested by the brain.

#6: Visualization and Imagination

Fortunately, the subconscious does not distinguish between real and imagined experiences. Because of this, you can intentionally regulate your subjective mind. When visualization is done correctly, the subconscious mind will never argue with you, think you don't have it or think you haven't made the change.

The subconscious mind works through sound, taste, smell, touch, sight, and emotions rather than language. All of our experiences consist of thought, sensation, and emotion. This is how the mind remembers and interprets events. Consider the sensation of touching a hot burner with your hand. When you think of the word lemon, you might picture a lemon, or you might be able to feel, smell, or taste one. This is your subconscious at its best. Take note of how simple this is.

Remember, your subconscious mind cannot distinguish between fantasy and reality. As a result, the more specific your images are, the more information you are feeding your subconscious mind. This leads to a beneficial shift in behavior. Our conscious mind has a penchant for focusing on and visualizing past events, which are frequently unfavorable. Visualizing your desired outcome in the now, with all of the sensations and feelings you can conjure up, deceives your subconscious into believing it is already happening.

The subconscious mind can see the larger picture and isn't confined to what has already transpired. This means that if you can honestly "see" yourself as successful in your mind, your subconscious will accept it as fact. Athletes are known to utilize visualization to improve their performance, but anyone can do it. Visualization is so powerful, in fact, that psycho-neuromuscular theory claims that simply envisioning exercising your muscles can make them stronger.

Get into a peaceful and comfortable mindset while visualizing. Consider what your life would be like if all of your wishes and desires were fulfilled. It's critical to concentrate solely on the desired end product rather than how it came about. Rather than watching yourself, immerse yourself in the visualization and imagine it from a first-person perspective. Most crucial, during your visualization process, train your mind to absorb as many different sensation states as possible. Smell the air, look around you at the environment and the people you're with, touch things, be aware of your gait as you walk, taste your favorite meal, and listen to the sounds. As previously said, your subconscious mind is fluent in the language of feelings. The more you assimilate these sensations during this process, the more your subconscious mind will seek their expression and actualization.

#7: **Expectation**

Expectations have the power to dominate your life and create self-fulfilling prophecies. Your subconscious mind's overarching plan is based on expectation. Your notion that you are a specific type of person with a particular position creates the expectations that determine whether you are successful or not. Expectations may either energize you to accomplish more or leave you discouraged and disappointed. Unfortunately, many people's expectations are shaped by their early life experiences. Finding strategies to adjust your expectations, on the other hand, is necessary if you want to make positive changes to your reality.

The brain stores thousands of your habitual activities, making them easily retrievable by your subconscious mind. Combination patterns are recognized by all nerve cells. When they fail to perceive a pattern, any cells unrelated to your current worry become blocked. Neural circuits throughout the nervous system turn off other circuits when their sections are activated. As a result, context is discovered by eliminating variables. This is how everything you do works. This eliminates all words from your vocabulary that do not fit the expression of your thoughts. As a result, unless you are repeatedly challenged to establish new expectations, your range of expectations will be constrained.

When the mind is confronted with a "perceived" unfavorable life scenario, it can be challenging to maintain a cheerful outlook. Because it is a survival mechanism, it is prone to making negative assumptions or projections about the scenario. This is where remaining open to the mind's movements without becoming too involved with it can come in handy . This approach will prevent your vibration from being entirely influenced by the mind's negativity, allowing new expectations and solutions to emerge without coercion.

Begin to transform your expectations into more pleasant anticipations by removing any negative assumptions your mind has delivered to you. Allow these assumptions to exist as they are, and then let them go without attaching any negative or positive feelings to them. The best attitude is to never arrive at a negative conclusion about anything that happens and instead consider everything as a step toward a more positive reality. This condition of open positive expectation is powerful and keeps you in sync with your life-stream, allowing solutions and desired realities to develop quickly.

Furthermore, cultivating self-assurance and triumphs will automatically lead to reasonable expectations. This is why you need to tell your mind continuously that you are already doing these things. One method to do this is to become actively aware of anything in life that brings you joy, no matter how insignificant it may seem. Expectation releases dopamine and energizes you. You may train your brain to automatically begin looking for greater happiness by intentionally observing the things that make you happy. As a result, the subjective mind develops new expectations.

#8: Let Go of How Your Desires Will Manifest

The strength of expectations goes hand in hand with "how" something happens. The mind will never understand why an event occurred, just as it will never be able to comprehend the full context of how something will unfold in the future. It simply seeks out and attracts variables. When a person has high expectations for how a specific outcome should occur but then sees something different, this can create a sense of disappointment or anxiety, which can sabotage what is being accomplished in their favor.

If, on the other hand, that person allows themselves to stay in a place of positive expectation without drawing any negative conclusions about how a particular event should unfold, they will remain resistance-free, allowing their subconscious mind to manifest a reality that is far better than what their conscious mind could imagine. What appears unfavorable to the mind is sometimes part of the process of transforming into a more positive reality. The most powerful technique to allow well-being to consistently flow into your reality is to avoid negative judgments while remaining in a place of positive expectation in all situations.

Because the mind is wired to solve problems, letting go of how things turn out can seem counter-intuitive. Learning to surrender to that process, on the other hand, releases any resistance that the mind tries to build. Recognize that your mind has neither the capacity nor the need to know about the issue's plethora of subtleties and complexities to accomplish the job.

Furthermore, the previously described mechanisms support mentally living in an "as if it's already mine" state. Before you can have your want, you must feel as if you already have it. The "how" becomes irrelevant once this happens, since the mind believes the outcome of the request being fulfilled. The subconscious mind doesn't need to retain the "how" it happened because it doesn't matter at that moment. It simply "is." This displays the level of faith required to bring about miracles in one's life.

#9: Meditation

Allowing our left/logical brain to step aside creates space for the right brain's reality to emerge, bringing more balance and joy into our awareness and our lives. The subconscious mind resides in the right hemisphere of the brain. We activate the right brain through meditation, while the left brain goes into a condition of rest. The right brain is then given more room to shine. If we lay our wishes and intentions in this place, we will manifest and create more effectively. This helps balance both hemispheres of the brain and gives us more power. In other words, making conscious decisions to work on your manifestations permits the subconscious mind to take control.

If you've never tried meditation before, simply sit in a peaceful spot, close your eyes, and take a few deep, long breaths to calm your mind and body. Allow your ideas to come in at random intervals and then drift away without emotional attachment. Begin to pay attention to your natural breathing. If you find yourself slipping into your thinking mode, gently bring your attention back to your breathing. As your breathing becomes more rhythmic and your physical body relaxes, the number of ideas rolling around in your mind will gradually decrease. Focus your undivided attention on your goal. Whatever you concentrate on in this condition will be imprinted straight onto your subconscious.

Meditation is a type of sleep in which you are aware of your surroundings. Scientists have discovered evidence that people who meditate are more aware of their unconscious brain activity, resulting in a feeling of conscious control over their bodies and their surroundings. Meditation aids in gaining creative energy for what you aim to accomplish, just as sleeping aids in gaining energy for daily functioning. It allows a person to actively tap into the power of their subconscious mind to achieve goals. It has been shown to help people achieve a higher level of consciousness, increased attention, creativity, self-awareness, and to reach a more relaxed and serene state of mind.

When you meditate regularly, the part of the brain that continuously refers back to you, your perspective and experiences, and the strong, firmly-held link to bodily sensation and the fear centers, starts to break down. As this link fades, there is no longer any presumption that a sensation or a fleeting feeling of dread indicates that something is wrong or that the self is the source of the problem. As you begin to dissolve that connection, your capacity to disregard worry symptoms improves, resulting in a more pleasant, healthy, and reasonable subconscious mind.

With time and practice, people become calmer, have a better capacity for empathy, and respond to things, people, and events in their lives in a more balanced way. When it comes to wishes, this activity communicates a frequency conducive to positive outcomes. Nevertheless, everyday practice is necessary to sustain the new brain connections that develop as a result of meditation. Remember that there are a variety of contemplative techniques to choose from, and each person should choose what works best for them.

#10: **Become a Conscious Receiver**

Teaching your subconscious mind that you are a receiver of the things you seek is one of the most effective ways to achieve what you want. You must send out the message that you are deserving of all you desire and then be receptive to receiving it. Imagine having an antenna in your mind that can send and receive vibrations to deliver your demands to you. Your mind similarly employs vibrations like a radio receiver, which uses an antenna to capture radio waves, processes the ones that vibrate at the proper frequency, and then transmits the sound through speakers.

If you have feelings of being worthless, not good enough, alienated, and unlovable, this is not your absolute truth. The truth is that you were born worthy and perfect, and there is nothing you can do, be, or have that can change that. Such notions are relics of the past.

Surprisingly, the vast majority of people are better senders than receivers, because giving brings a person immense delight or serves as a mental reward. Receiving is a skill that takes time to master. It necessitates intimacy and tolerance. Being a good receiver also honors the giver by providing them with the joy of watching you receive. There's nothing wrong with receiving; in fact, all of existence wants to rejoice in our happiness at being able to do so. Furthermore, the more we are able to receive, the more we can give back.

Receiving praise graciously and without deflecting back to the other person is an excellent way to practice. Say "thank you" and realize that you will be uncomfortable at first. This may seem strange, but after a few times, you will notice that you are becoming less anxious and more appreciative of the compliments and of yourself. Your mind will be able to break down a barrier because of this.

When something positive happens in your life, acknowledge it and express gratitude. Gratitude is accepting that what is happening gives you joy and that it's okay to get more. It also shows that you are conscious that you are a recipient of good fortune. If you appreciate what you already have, you will be able to obtain more. Based on the feeling states involved, the subconscious mind will diligently search for more of what pleases you. Rather than focusing on what you don't have, be grateful for what you do have, whether they be situations, relationships, items, or even difficulties. They assist you in growing and manifesting more of what you seek.

Tell yourself "I am worthy" as many times as you can until it becomes a habit. The more you utilize this auto-suggestion, the more the truth of that phrase will be revealed to your subconscious mind. Be dedicated to achieving your goals, and remember that the universe is on your side. Most importantly, practice ways to love yourself without needing others' approval. More of what you love comes to you as a result of your loving energy.

Practice, practice, practice...

It's takes practice to manipulate your subconscious mind for your benefit. In other words, if you actually want to alter your life, you will need to invest time and effort. A subconscious mind is a powerful tool with limitless potential, and anyone may reprogram it to operate in their favor or else remain a slave to its earlier training. You open yourself to new experiences and opportunities in your life by allowing your belief systems to be transformed. This also makes it easier for your intentions to materialize.

Recognize that your emotions and thoughts are nothing more than pure, intense energy. What you think in your head, feel in your body, and believe directly impacts what you attract. As a result, we each have the potential to channel good energy into our minds to create the life we want. All of us can employ this vast mental capacity to create enormous wealth, lose weight, and have fulfilling relationships, a healthy body, and overall enjoyable experiences. By merely touching the power of their subconscious, people have miraculously recovered from terminal illnesses and produced great wealth for themselves.

Your conscious mind is a gardener, capable of growing whatever you plant. It chooses which seeds to utilize and plants them in your subconscious mind's garden. Simply cover the seeds gently and water them every day. Beneath the soil, the seed reacts with the magnificent, fertile earth of subjective consciousness. A seedling will sprout and seek the sun if the gardener continues to support it through deliberate effort. This extraordinary creative movement takes place in your subconscious mind. All of your desires will flourish if you properly care for them.

4

SURRENDER - THE SECRET TO THE LAW OF ATTRACTION

In Zen Buddhism, the term Shoshin means "beginner's mind." The central idea behind this concept is that we should remain open and assume nothing as we move through life's experience. Having preconceived notions or attaching to our ideas blocks us from maintaining a receptive state. For example, if someone sees themselves as an 'expert,' they are less likely to take in or even consider new information. For such a person to receive new information or experiences, they need to set aside their identity as an 'expert.' One cannot receive if they are unwilling to let go.

Have you ever tried to hug someone when you're holding bags in both hands? It isn't easy. Similarly, many people carry baggage around when it comes to life, and when a new opportunity arrives, they can't embrace it. We can carry only so much with us before we block the infinite gifts life offers us—whether these gifts are opportunities, people, intuitive hunches, creative ideas, or even new positive perspectives and feelings. If we don't let go of our old thoughts and emotions, they will keep us from experiencing new ones.

In other words, if we constantly think the same thoughts and feel the same emotions, we attract the same kinds of circumstances into our lives. To change this, we need to be open to letting go of the old so that we can embrace the new.

LET GO OF THE OLD TO INVITE IN THE NEW

One thing that should be apparent by now is that an intelligent force exists beyond what we usually perceive. There are possibilities our limited minds can never imagine. This concept is called "Bounded Rationality." Human beings can only come up with a limited number of solutions to a problem before they run out of options. However, the invisible field surrounding us is not bound by the mind's rationality; it is infinite. Once we understand the limitlessness of our potential, we can (slowly but surely) begin to embrace it.

Surely it's more efficient to put faith in a limitless source than to keep insisting on a limited one, right? Often, when someone has a positive manifesting experience, it might not be exactly what they'd imagined—it could be similar but it could also be completely different. This is why we need to be willing to let go of the singular path we are on and allow ourselves to pivot when necessary to recognize and embrace the other, better possibilities that can show up for us.

Once we begin to alter our state by using the principles and exercises in this book, we realize that we can no longer accept things at face value. When I 'got' this, I was startled at how quickly I was manifesting and how effortless and synchronistic life became. Things that, on the surface, looked negative, had an underlying 'force' that propelled me toward a positive outcome. This happened because I could experience beyond my senses, think beyond my assumptions, and choose beyond my (supposed) limited options.

How does this work? Think, for example, of a person who is walking through a forest, happily enjoying peace and calm. Suddenly, they trip over a root, fall, and rip their new pants. But as they pick themselves up, they notice a large gold nugget lying on the ground in front of them. If they hadn't tripped, they never would have seen the nugget. Instead of lamenting about their torn pants, now they have the means to purchase a whole new wardrobe!

When you begin to apply the principle of letting go, things like this will start to happen to you (hopefully not the falling-down part!) at an ever-increasing rate. The only way it won't work is if you build up resistance to what you want. Remember, reality manifests based on what you are resonating with vibrationally at any moment in time. Therefore, if you do not have faith that something is possible, well, it never will be, because it's not a possibility you are willing to consider or become aware of. If you identify with what is in front of you and believe you need to move along a predetermined path to achieve success, your attitudes and limited belief systems will always create resistance towards what you want to manifest. But once you commit to trusting what lies beyond your current perception, you begin to trust the unknown. This is the first step in putting your faith in the universe. When we surrender our limitations, we become aligned with the unlimited.

Surrendering Who You Think You Are

Negativity exists all around us. We see it in the news. We hear it on the radio. We watch it in entertainment and on social media. We spend our childhoods being told what not to do and what cannot be done. Society does not ask us to "live our true nature" or "follow our excitement." Rather, we are told to "fit in" and "follow the course."

> *"Children learn that answers are more important than questions, and conforming is more critical than originality and self-expression."*
> —Michael J. Gelb

Because of this, often, we find ourselves on a path that doesn't resonate with what our hearts truly want. The longer we stay on this path, the more difficult it becomes to break free from conditioned thoughts and emotions. But here is where we need to assert ourselves. If someone were to say to you, "I demand that you feel unhappy," what would your reply be? You would most certainly tell them that the way you feel is your decision.

Why would you not exercise that same choice when it comes to how you perceive things? Once you understand that nothing in the universe is ever set in stone, why give negativity any credence at all? Since all possible realities exist in the universe, why focus on the negative aspects that favor you least? You cannot change reality, but you can respond to it. Your response is what creates your reality.

In essence, by surrendering control over who you think you need to be, you give yourself permission to create your life experience based on your alignment—and nothing else. You must let go of who you unconsciously think you are and begin aligning consciously with who you really are. This is essential if you wish to welcome a reality that aligns with your already abundant, joyful, limitless nature.

So, what does it mean to "let go?" Here is an exercise to help.

EXERCISE: SURRENDERING TO INFINITY

To facilitate your empowerment, consider the following practices.

Let go of physical attachments. We hold on to material items, relationships, and jobs in the name of "tradition" or "security." The truth is, it is easy to stay the same and complain about not experiencing change because we identify with what we currently have. The idea of change threatens our current identity, or ego-self.

Empty your cup of ideas to refill it with something better. Are you attached to beliefs, ideas, or ways of being? Are you filled with assumptions about how your life ought to be? If so, there could be an internal blockage that keeps you from accepting new thoughts or adopting new perspectives. To change this, begin by adopting a 'beginner's mind,' the Zen Buddhist term explained at the opening of this chapter. Only then will you be able to tune in to the infinite perspectives of your physical experience and begin changing your responses to it.

Let go of how you think others should perceive you. One of the best examples of this can be seen on social media. There is nothing wrong with social media platforms, but identifying with who you appear to be there can result in unnecessary anxiety and stress. Many people would rather focus on how others see them than create their dream reality in real-life. The opinions of others can be similar to incoming negative thoughts. Observe them; do not engage with them.

Let go of other people's expectations. Consider those who expect you to do and be what they think would be best for you. Often, these expectations come from those closest to you, family, friends, or partners. The fact is, only you can decide what is best for you. Nobody has all the answers. Listening to the insight, advice, and new perspectives given to you by those you trust is a great way to start you thinking, but your intuition should always take precedence at the end of the day.

Let go of assumptions about how you think you need to act and be. Within your subconscious, there exists a wide range of conditioning that says, in essence, "In order to achieve XYZ, you must do ABC." We match these expectations with our hopes and dreams as we create our reality throughout our lives. But when we build resistance to alignment and force ourselves to follow these arbitrary patterns, problems arise. Expand your perspective, and new doors will begin to open up for you.

Let go of how you believe you need to feel and think. We all have conditioned responses that match the events in our lives. However, when we allow ourselves to become a prisoner of these conditioned thoughts and feelings, we limit ourselves to a predetermined 'script' for how we should respond to situations. When we commit to changing our reality, we also change these old mental and emotional scripts.

Let go of your attachment to what is. When you choose to change your life experience, everything changes. This includes the things you own as well as the relationships you have. Some will change a lot, some very little. If you fear change and try to hold on to the familiar, things will remain the same. Mastering the Laws of Manifestation implies that you have the ability to enact change. Rather than tightening your grip on what currently exists, allow change to happen!

The essence of letting go is moving beyond the narrow, single path of your current existence and opening yourself up to an infinite number of new pathways. To attract the things you truly want in your life, you must be ready to feel and act according to those desires. This new form of attraction entails letting go of your resistance to change and making peace with everything in your life. When you're ready to say, "I understand how things are, and I accept it; however, I intend to change it," you will be open to allowing new things to manifest in your life.

> "Change happens when the pain of staying the same is greater than that of change."
> —Tony Robbins

As you can see, ironically, to be empowered is to surrender. I'm not referring to the type of surrender that involves waving a white flag and giving up on your desires. I am talking about releasing the resistance that stops you from obtaining your desires.

Surrendering involves being at peace with what is. This peace must come from the knowledge that where you are currently is the beginning of the journey that will take you to where you want to go. Many people mistakenly push against the things they feel they don't want. For example, some people feel they have lost something and fear losing even more. But, by comparing what they once had to what they have now, they are merely holding on to the past and resisting the present. This is not 'letting go.'

Another mistake people make is comparing what they have now to what they want for their future. This is also not 'letting go.' As long as we view our current situation negatively, we will continue to attract circumstances that match it. When we embrace our current situation, knowing that it is a starting point on a new journey, we allow the universe to assist us in manifesting our desires. Rather than intending to improve our manifestation abilities, we ought instead to let go of what holds us back and choose to receive new experiences.

EXERCISE: THE LETTING GO PROCESS

The letting go process can be broken down into three steps:

1. Acknowledgment

Refusing to acknowledge your current circumstances is simply a form of ignoring the reality you wish to change. Change cannot occur unless there is a starting point. How can you intend to manifest a better situation if you refuse to acknowledge the one you are currently in? In a way, this is a form of self-delusion led by the ego-self. The ego-self defines its existence and worth based on what it is experiencing physically. Thus, if circumstances are not ideal, it will look for the why. This is when we blame others and play the victim, and holds true for every aspect and area of life.

As such, when feelings of sadness, guilt, anger, frustration, victimization, etc., are present, we need to acknowledge them. Trying to escape from your feelings will only suppress them—and when we suppress our feelings long enough, they begin to control our lives from within the unconscious parts of our minds and bodies.

2. Acceptance

The second stage of letting go is to accept this truth: you are a human being, and human beings have emotions. There is no reason to view your emotions in a way that disempowers you. Feeling guilty, ashamed, or frustrated about how you feel are just a few examples of emotions that can disempower us.

Problems arise when we attach ourselves to negative emotions and allow them to define our experiences. For example, when we feel sad, it's common to create the story that we are sad people. But when we define ourselves in this way, ultimately, we are 'boxing in' what is and creating resistance around it. What if, within the negative experience, there is a lesson to be learned? Wouldn't learning the lesson make the experience more valuable? Of course it would. This is how the universe works—it is always in the process of creating disorder, chaos, and ultimately, change. Change is normal. Discomfort and chaos lead to growth and novelty. This is what manifesting is all about.

The bottom line? You need to give yourself permission to feel however you are feeling, without judging yourself or your emotions. The more order you try to place upon a given process, the more resistance you build. Allow your emotions to exist, because whatever you are feeling shines a light on your unconscious perspectives and beliefs. View your emotions as beacons, and you will no longer feel the need to run away or allow your feelings to hold you back.

3. Making the Choice

The final stage of letting go is making the choice to do so. You must choose to let go of your past conditioned emotions. Old emotions are anchors that keep you stuck in an old identity. When you make this choice, you refuse to feed the ego-self. You must make this intention because by doing so, in effect, you choose to let go of everything in your life that correlates with those old emotions.

The way to make this choice is by disidentifying with the emotion you wish to let go of. Disidentifying means to disown, and that which we do not own cannot affect us. This is how we create the internal space needed for change.

The second part of this step is to question your emotions. When you ask yourself questions, you become conscious of your unconscious, thereby bringing pent-up emotions to the surface.

Everyone is different and will therefore see results within a different time frame, depending on the intensity and quantity of their suppressed emotions. However, we can all start by asking four simple questions:

1. Am I willing to allow this emotion to come up?
2. Am I willing to feel this emotion fully, without judgment?
3. Am I willing to let go of this emotion?
4. When am I willing to let go of this emotion?

Once you commit to letting go of emotions that no longer serve you, you are also letting go of people, places, and things that keep you out of alignment. These can come in the form of an abusive relationship, a negative social circle, expectations of others, or fear of failure. So, you might ask yourself, "How will I know when I have finally let go?" You can lay this question to rest by asking yourself these final two questions:

1. Am I okay with letting go of the people, places, and things that keep me out of alignment?
2. Am I okay with not manifesting my desire in the way I expect to?

By asking (and answering) these questions, you will be able to determine whether you are still attached to your current circumstances, desires, and expectations. This is also an excellent litmus test that will tell you if you're genuinely embodying the version of you that resonates with your desired reality. Remember, before we can have, we must do, but before we can do, we must be.

If you answered "yes" to both of these questions, you are well on your way to increasing your receptivity and activating the 'receiving mode.' This is the mode in which you are open to manifesting new and unknown creations and experiences.

Choosing to be (and being) proficient at letting go is an excellent way to recalibrate your frequency and alter your path toward more meaningful goals. Lingering and dwelling on the past brings stagnant energy, which keeps you feeling stuck and resistant toward what you truly want.

If you answered "no" to either of these two final questions, you need to uncover the hidden beliefs and perspectives that are holding you back. Fortunately, by following the suggestions outlined in this book, that task should not be difficult. After you have identified the issue, you're free to work on letting it go and manifest from a place of freedom rather than from one of limitation.

5

PRACTICING THE LAW OF ATTRACTION

Understanding all the laws related to the Law of Attraction will give you more in-depth insight into how you can use them to change your life for the better. Once you grasp how they work, you can apply these laws to everything you do in life and change your habits.

THE LAW OF MANIFESTATION

This law states that if you focus on something hard enough, it will manifest in your life. The things in your dominant thoughts will eventually find their way to the physical world. If you think more about positive things, you will get more of them in life, too.

If you want your thoughts and desires to become a reality, you must first believe you can achieve them and feel good about them. Once you start feeling good and maintain that feeling, you will find yourself at a frequency where you are open to receiving good things. The express lane to that frequency is to keep verbalizing that you receive what you ask for. For it to work, you must "feel it" intensely, as if you have already received it.

The universe acts fast in manifesting what you ask for. You can blame yourself for the delay in getting to the right frequency; the place where you believe and feel that you already have what you are thinking of and longing for. It takes the same amount of time for the universe to manifest one million dollars as one dollar. You just thought it should take much longer to come up with a million dollars than it takes to come up with one.

This chapter will explore some concrete exercises to help jump-start the manifestation process. For starters, begin thinking about what you want, talk about it, write it down, and give it energy, attention, and focus. Just say, "I am in the process of…" and imagine your desire becoming true to help you feel good and emit positive vibrations. If you prefer, you can also say, "I am in the process of earning more from my business," or, "I am in the process of becoming healthy" to manifest those claims.

When a statement rings true for you, it makes you feel good. This positive feeling will send a positive vibration that the Law of Attraction will process and respond to by beckoning to more positive things. This is how the Law of Manifestation works, and you can begin using it now.

THE LAW OF MAGNETISM

The Law of Attraction never stops working, which means that you are a magnet 24/7 to everything you have ever thought. If you are not careful about what dominates your thoughts, you might attract the wrong things and bring about negativity in your life.

You are the universe's most powerful magnet. That power comes from your thoughts. Aside from their magnetic properties, thoughts also work at a frequency. Every thought you make is released to the universe and attracts things with the same frequency releasing the same vibration before returning.

The prevailing thought, which 'New Thought' movement proponents call "one's mental attitude," acts like a magnet. Whatever that mental attitude is, it will attract conditions of the same nature. So, if you wish to change your circumstances, change your thoughts.

How do you change your mental attitude? Change the mental images in your brain. If you do not like what you see now, destroy those images and create new ones. Then, start using the power of visualization. Picture what you want and hold on to that picture until it comes true.

Do you want to stop smoking? Put the Law of Magnetism to work. Visualize yourself as a non-smoker whose hands are always in your pockets. Imagine yourself doing something other than holding a cigarette. Picture how wonderful it feels to be smoke-free. Think about all the benefits of stopping smoking, including improved health, a better sense of smell, saving money, and more.

Do you want to lose weight? If you have dropped countless New Year's resolutions about this because you failed to follow through, this time try applying the Law of Magnetism. Imagine being your slimmer and healthier self. Think about the clothes you will wear with confidence and look forward to the activities you will be able to do without running out of breath. Visualize how great you look after losing weight. Soon enough, that vision will come true, thanks to the Law of Magnetism.

THE LAW OF UNWAVERING DESIRE

This principle states that only doubt-free and stable intentions manifest. Regardless of whether they are good or bad, your intentions should be precise. They should not be clouded by doubt, worry, desperation, or fear. The strength and firmness of your desire determine how fast it will come to fruition. Focus on it, keep thinking about how you can achieve it, and believe that you have achieved it. With unwavering desire comes the need for unwavering faith, too.

The moment you genuinely believe that you are worthy of what you desire, it will come true. If you want the Law of Unwavering Desire to start working its magic:

1. Avoid envisioning the possibility of failing.
2. Erase all doubts and anything that causes doubt to develop in the first place.
3. Train yourself not to doubt, and you will be well on your way to getting what you desire.

If you have fallen short of your goals before due to a lack of persistence, intensify your desire. Weak desires can only return weak results. As we know, the sun cannot fully shine when it's cloudy, so don't let your doubts cloud your intentions. Envision the things that you want as if they are already yours. Claim with 100 percent certainty that you deserve what you desire.

But even your purest desire is not enough. When you pray and express your sincerest desire, you should believe that God can give you what you are asking for. Believe that God is ready to provide what you truly desire. When you pray, do it the Psalmists' way. Ask for what you want, then eliminate all doubts and fears by affirming His willingness and power to grant your prayers.

THE LAW OF DELICATE BALANCE

The Law of Attraction works best if everything is in balance, and balance only occurs when you enjoy what you have right now but look forward to the goals you have for the future. You need to focus on your goals, but you should not cross the line into desperation, obsession, or anxiousness. Don't undervalue your present because you are desperately looking forward to the future.

When we try to attract things with desperation, we attract negative energy. We may repel the people and circumstances that could have helped us. Appreciate what you have now. Imagine the appreciation you will feel upon realizing your goals, then focus on that sense of gratitude instead.

Desperation is a negative emotion that you do not want to associate with. It sends the wrong signals and draws the wrong things to you. Learn how to balance your dreams for the future with what is happening in your life right now. Be happy and satisfied with what you have now while holding on to what the future will bring.

The moment you become too anxious, you manifest fear and distress. This sense of desperation will cause you to act like an overeager child. You just planted a seed, but you want to keep checking on it to see if it has taken root or not. But the constant digging will stop the seed from germinating and growing. Give the seed enough time and room to grow, and your patience will eventually pay off.

If you follow the Law of Delicate Balance, you should learn to leave that seed alone. That does not mean ignoring it, though. As you allow the seed time to germinate, you should continue to strive, being productive and working to create new opportunities for yourself.

THE LAW OF HARMONY

Like everything else in the universe, you are linked to billions of other energy sources. These might be invisible connections, but trust that they are there. The Law of Harmony reminds us that we can become a potent energy source if we align with the universe and our surroundings. Everything is connected, and we find power by tapping into that connection, much like how a single drop of water derives strength when dropped into the ocean.

When you are in harmony with the universe, your desires and energy source will put you closer to the doors of universal abundance, giving you access to powers you never dreamed of tapping into before. Practice aligning yourself with the universe to open and keep the universal flow going smoothly.

More than thinking about your goals in life, you need to consciously and systematically direct your thoughts toward those goals. Only then can you say that you have aligned yourself in harmony with the Universal Mind and the Infinite. Once you achieve harmony, your body automatically becomes in tune with the Infinite. In turn, it opens the Universal Mind's creative power. This creative power will help manifest the object of your desires.

THE LAW OF RIGHT ACTION

We all regularly face situations in which we must choose between right and wrong, and this will either bring us positive or negative energy. The Law of Right Action, or Conscientious Action, states that how you treat others will return to your life in the same way. If you keep doing the right thing, you can expect positive things to come your way.

This law states that if you value and respect others, you can draw the same value and respect back into your life. This is why it is important to consciously think about whether something you do will bring you positive things or not. Consider whether it will respect and honor others the way you want to be respected and honored yourself. Ask yourself if it will bring something good to the universe in the way you expect to receive good from it.

When engaging in the Right Action, you must maintain accountability for what you do, think, and desire. Remember that if you value yourself, you also need to value others. Focus on improving your physical, mental, spiritual, and emotional well-being. Eventually, you will learn how to pursue a conscientious life.

Before you do anything:

1. Ask if the action enhances your well-being.
2. Consider whether or not it shows respect to you, because if it does, it will be easier to show respect to others.
3. Think about whether the action shows compassion.

Everything that you do should speak of truth, but with tact. Preserve your dignity without blaming anyone or anything else. Conscientious living is about looking after other people's welfare without compromising your own.

One study that sought to establish the Behavioral Indicators of Conscientiousness explored just what conscientious people do. It defined conscientiousness as a personality trait that follows social norms, delays gratification, stays goal-directed, sets plans, and obeys the rules. The study also showed how this trait is associated with lower criminal activity, better health, and better social, economic, and workplace outcomes.

The study concluded that conscientious people exhibit self-control and goal achievement. It showed that conscientious people are clean and tidy hard workers and tend to think before acting. They follow social decorum and society's rules and are organized. They also tend to stand up straight, comb their hair, and note important dates. They also do things like polish their footwear and scrub floors. Those less conscientious tend to watch more television, exceed their credit limit, cancel plans, break promises, oversleep, and swear.

Another study showed why conscientious adults do well in subjective and objective success. At work, conscientious people complete tasks efficiently, work hard, and stay organized. They act responsibly and make careful decisions, making them more productive than others. These same behaviors help conscientious adults foster healthy relationships, promoting subjective well being while avoiding unnecessary conflicts and mending rifts.

In terms of health, those who are more conscientious tend to stay healthier. As a result, they have fewer absences and lower medical expenses. This tends to benefit them income-wise. These individuals also tend to be happier, probably because they do better in school. This academic success helps them acquire better-paying jobs, and can lead to greater subjective happiness.

THE LAW OF UNIVERSAL INFLUENCE

The Law of Universal Influence states that your positivity can affect everyone around you, regardless of whether you know them or not. It creates a ripple effect over your surroundings. For this reason, it is essential to be more aware of how you behave if you do not want to negatively influence other people. Always remember that you have an impact on your family, your work, and your social relationships, no matter how small that impact may seem.

Universal influence is at work whenever we enter a room where people are arguing, and we can feel the tension in the air, the energy created by the minds in conflict. Perhaps you have even seen it at work. You may feel excited, only to then be discouraged by other people's less enthusiastic reactions. You lose that excitement and wonder why you were excited in the first place.

The Law of Universal Influence shows us how to live our life as positively as we can, even while knowing that we might encounter negativity from other people. But we all have the power to prevent this energy from bringing us down. Simply direct your thoughts toward the positive rather than the negative.

One study showed that a happy worker is a productive worker. It suggests that organizations can benefit from setting up work environments that foster better moods. It also indicates that minimal positive psychology interventions may increase employees' happiness levels. This supports the idea that your positivity will help you and your organization succeed.

Now that you understand how these Laws of Attraction work, you can start changing your thinking habits for a better life. It all begins with knowing that you can affect your life and the lives around you.

These laws show us that our thoughts manifest in the outside world, and we attract the contents of those thoughts. They remind us not to have doubts about achieving our goals. They also teach us to appreciate the present and not be desperate about the future. They remind us that we are connected to everything in the universe, and that we need to do the right thing and be conscious of our influence on others.

HOW DO YOU APPLY THE LAW OF ATTRACTION TO REAL LIFE?

Be sure of what you want.

The first step is to be clear about what you want. Although you may think this is something everybody knows for themselves, do not skip this step. Too often, we only think we want something. What we genuinely desire may be significantly different from what we think we want. How so? We are taught what we should wish for, what we should become, and what we should do with our lives. But even if we achieve those things, it can turn out that they were not what our soul wanted. So, take some time to reflect on what you really want. Is it your own wish, or did someone else tell you that you should wish for it? Would it make you happy? Deep inside, you already know the answer. Be honest with yourself and let the real answers be heard.

For example, you may think you wish to finish your law studies. But maybe that's something your parents want, while you would rather become a writer. Or maybe your current priority is to get married and start a family, but your deepest desire is to ride a bike around the world. We must be honest with ourselves.

Ask the universe for help.

I mentioned this earlier. It is a huge benefit to know the mighty universe has your back. If you believe you are divinely protected and being guided toward your highest good, nothing can stop you. Simply ask the universe to give you what you want. You can either ask it out loud or say it in your mind – whatever's most comfortable for you. It's okay to conceptualize your request as a prayer. If you are more comfortable with a pen and paper, write a letter. The point is to ask the universe, for real, in any way you prefer. If the universe had a phone or an email address, even that would work. Afterward, behave as if you have ordered something from a shop and wait for your manifestation to arrive. Be excited. Be happy. Be patient. Be full of faith.

Write down your dreams.

The word abracadabra is believed to come from a Hebrew phrase that means, "I will create as I speak," or from the Aramaic, "I create like the word." The fact is, some kind of magic happens when we write. It has been scientifically proven that written goals have more of a chance of becoming a reality than oral goals. The same thing applies to wishes we want to manifest. When writing, our conscious and subconscious minds focus on our thoughts, and our energy flows where our attention goes. All of these are tools for attraction. Besides, written words on paper are a kind of first material manifestation of an idea. So, if you have written something down, you have already manifested it in one way, no matter how small. This begins the transition from the immaterial to the material world.

So, get a pen and paper and have fun writing out your new life scenario. Set your imagination free, and do not limit yourself. The only criteria should be good feelings.

Feel it.

It is not enough to keep an eye on your thoughts and carefully select them. Even creatively writing your new story is not enough. The crucial thing is to feel it. You will attract those things on the same vibration as your feelings. When you feel great, you fly high and attract extraordinary manifestations like a magnet. In short, you are creating with your feelings. Imagination and thoughts are given to you to cause emotions, which determines your vibration. So, imagine how you would feel if your wish were to come true. Try to feel as if it has already happened. These emotions will help you attract more of the same feelings by bringing wanted manifestations into your reality. Remember, it is not important what you do, but how you feel. Do whatever makes you feel wonderful. And choose your thoughts wisely, selecting only those that make you feel good.

What should you do with your beliefs?

We all believe many things about life and the world. Many of them are correct and useful. For example, it is dangerous to play with fire. This is a rational thought. Our beliefs can be supportive, such as when we think we are gorgeous and talented. In reasonable doses, this is good for our self-esteem. But, not all of our beliefs are lovely, supportive, or rational. While most adults no longer believe that Santa Claus exists, for some reason, we still believe other silly things we were taught as children. You can use positive thinking and mindfulness, but you will not be successful if you have limiting beliefs working against you. Granted, we all have some limiting beliefs, but if we do not do anything about them, our autopilot will default to the base emotions and thoughts we had as a child.

For this reason, your beliefs need some special attention and decluttering. First, you need to be clear about what you believe. What do you think is undoubtedly true about life, yourself, other people, and the world? What do you think about love, friendship, and family? What do you think about money and work? How do you feel about all of these topics? Take as much time as you need for deep introspection and reflection on each of those themes. Dig deep into your beliefs and see if they serve you. A belief is helpful if it is true, rational, supportive, or makes you feel good. It is not useful if it limits, sabotages, or discourages you. It is time to get rid of toxic beliefs and replace them with new ones.

Affirmations can help.

When you have realized that you need to change some of your beliefs, affirmations are your secret weapon. These are positive, declarative sentences. For this purpose, there is nothing more powerful. A good affirmation needs to be formulated in the present tense and, most often, in the first person. For example, "I am loved. I am peaceful. I am a money magnet." You can find numerous affirmations out there, but you could and should create your own. For every belief that you want to change, create a new one that is positive and supportive, and formulate it as an affirmation. Then you simply need to repeat it until you accept it as your new belief. The first hour in the morning and the last one before you fall asleep are perfect times for affirmations.

How does this work? Our subconscious does not judge and cannot differentiate true from false. It does not know the difference between what is real and what is imagined. Our beliefs are only the thoughts we choose to believe, often those repeated over and over in our heads. Everything that you continuously repeat becomes your belief and tends to prove itself. This is not magic; it is psychology. It is how our minds work and why affirmations can change your life. Just formulate what you want, repeat it again and again, and let the universe make it your new reality.

Connect with the vibrations that are best for you.

You already know from what we've discussed here that you need to raise your vibration to attract what you want. All methods and techniques for self-improvement and attraction have this in common--their primary purpose is to increase one's vibration. The only way to have a high vibration and maintain it is to feel good or, even better, to feel *great*. Everything you love to do or like to think about - everything that makes you happy - raises your vibration. You can raise yours by choosing only positive thoughts. For example, if you only think of things you adore, you will emit so many positive waves that all you want will hurry to reach you.

The basic techniques to raise your vibration are thought control (thinking in the best possible way by choosing only good thoughts), focusing with purpose, and gratefulness. So, if you want to feel better now, think about the things that make your life special and worthwhile. Think about your loved ones, the wonderfulness of the world, or watch funny animal videos. What is essential is how you feel, not what you do. Choose to do more of what makes you happy and adapt your schedule to those priorities, not the other way around. Focus intentionally on the bright side of everything. There is always a sunny side. Find it and hold on to it. And, finally, count your blessings. Consider how lucky you are and say thank you.

Use the power of focus.

Energy flows where attention goes. What you focus your attention on, grows. So, what things in your life do you want to grow and cultivate, and what things are better left out of your garden? Your focus functions like a camera lens. Be careful what you choose to include in your life movie. Focusing on what you like and what you would be glad to have more of in your reality makes you feel good. Everything will look better and, by the Law of Attraction, you will bring more similar experiences, things, and people to your life. I am not saying that you should ignore problems that demand action or attention. But there are many things that only deplete our energy. Focusing on them leaves us drained and in a bad mood--these are the things that should not be given a place in your movie. Put a mental "ignore" sign on them and change your focus. After some practice, you will be pleasantly surprised by how easy it is to shift your focus and be intentional in choosing your thoughts and feelings.

Gratefulness.

Being grateful is the most powerful and quickest way to improve vibrations. It is an instant way to feel good. It is easy, quick, totally free, and entirely under your control. The technique is incredible, and your job is to apply it. Think about all the things in your life you could be thankful for. What would you miss if you lost them? Be grateful for life, for your body, its parts, and its function. You can be thankful for your mind, your imagination, your intelligence, your brain, for beautiful days, sunlight, for all of the precious people in your life, for your bed, for a cup of coffee, for whatever makes your life easier or more enjoyable. Everyone alive has plenty to be grateful for and everything above and beyond those things is a bonus. We are fortunate to be here. But unfortunately, many of us are not aware of this.

Count your blessings whenever you can. Do it in the morning to raise your vibration for a new day, before bedtime to program your subconscious, or during the day just to feel good. When you are thankful for what you already have, you attract more of the same vibration. If you like to write thankful notes, even better. You can start a gratefulness diary or a happiness jar. These are exciting projects that will remind you every day to say thanks for what you have. And when the project is finished, they will remind you how lucky you are every time you look at them. For the happiness jar, you will need a big, empty jar and many little pieces of paper. Every day, write down one thing you are thankful for and put it in the jar. This is simple but effective. Your jar will be a reminder for you and a magnet to attract more pieces of paper with wonderful things written on them.

Practice creative visualization.

As we discussed earlier, our minds are ruled by our conscious mind and subconscious mind. We can be aware of that fact or not, but when our mind receives an order, it does not know or care where it comes from. That is why it can be tricky to understand all of our emotions and actions. But we can make use of this. Again, you will attract what you want most easily if you feel like it has already happened. Because our minds do not care if something is real or imagined, we can easily trick them. By visualizing your desired scenario, you will feel like it has already occurred. In this way, you will realize that you do not need the manifestation to achieve those emotions, and, more importantly, the universe will send you more reasons to stay on your current vibration.

This is the point of creative visualization. Imagine the scenario you want. Be creative and pay attention to details. Create a picture you believe. Your mind is clever; do not forget that. If you want to provoke feelings, you need to put in some effort and be imaginative. Imagine situations, things, people, reactions, smell, taste, touch, your actions, and your feelings. Imagine everything you can. All of this is needed to feel the emotion. Emotions are what vibrate and attract, so that is our goal. The point of creative visualization is to provoke adequate emotion, which will attract more of the same.

Trust the process and be patient.

Belief means that you trust even without seeing. Attraction is one of those things. Being suspicious and impatient will make you vibrate on an entirely different frequency than you should if you want to attract good. Being calm and believing everything you want is on the way makes you feel excited. Expect beautiful things to happen. If you believe that you are divinely protected and guided, you'll feel safe. If something does not happen, you'll know the obstacles are meant for a higher good. Remember, the universe answers your thoughts like a genie from a bottle. Whatever you choose to believe, it responds, "Let it be so." So, choose to have help, and everything will be much easier. Impatience is a sign that you do not believe. Be peaceful and wait patiently for your manifestation to become visible. Believing also means that you are sure that things will happen at the perfect time for you. There is no need to rush. The universe knows best when the time is right. Silence your ego a bit. You are not the one who knows what is best for you. You do not know what should happen, or how and when it will take place. Let the universe make those decisions. You must enjoy life in perfect harmony.

6

HOW SELF-SABOTAGE REDUCES THE EFFICIENCY OF THE LAW OF ATTRACTION

Self-sabotage shows up whenever you subconsciously prevent yourself from being successful. This is reflected in self-damaging behavior, which you consciously would never choose. You think, feel, and act in such a way that the success you desire has no chance to enter your life.

Why, for heaven's sake, would you ever want to do such a crazy thing, you may be asking yourself?

Let's take a closer look at this surprisingly perfectly normal behavior.

For starters, please don't judge yourself if you've ever acted this way. Chances are, you weren't even aware you were doing it. Accept that you probably always do your best, according to your current state of knowledge, consciousness, and life circumstances.

The main reasons for self-sabotage typically originate in our past. Since we have been carrying these reasons around for a while, we are usually not even aware that they exist.

I am talking about the unconscious dogmas and presumptions we develop as a child--about how the world, people, and relationships work, and our abilities and personal values.

You will not believe how strongly these dogmas and beliefs are still operating within you, staying undetected but determining your life.

Have you ever seen an autopilot, the device that automatically navigates an airplane towards its destination, in action? This is exactly how we work sometimes. Our beliefs guide us automatically toward certain and often subconscious goals. The problem is that these old and hidden goals, which were set a long time ago, don't fit us anymore.

From our parents and our surroundings, we adopted a lot of presumptions about life and ourselves; whether we are good enough and loveable, for example, and many of us feel there is something we need to achieve in order to be loved. When our parents say things like, "Nothing in life is free; you have to work hard for your successes," they form a perception of how the world works that we carry around with us and that we have likely been following throughout life.

What we believe in shows up in our life.

What we think determines what we experience.

Our thoughts are the filter through which life flows to us.

Everything you see and perceive around you mirrors your thoughts. You attract what you focus on. Change your thoughts, and your life will transform right in front of your eyes.

In addition to the beliefs we take from our families, there are also obligations we feel toward our ancestors.

Today we know that every family member has a particular role in the family system as a whole. This system works like a mobile crib that swings in a delicate equilibrium. If someone in the family falls out of the system through early death, accident, disease, or a bad marriage, someone else has to fill the gap. In many cases, guilt or certain destinies are adopted by descendants.

Imagine us as children being very loving and open-minded beings. Unfortunately, we also believe that it is our responsibility to make people around us happy. Children will do everything they can to make their parents happy, even when it's not their job and not working out well. As children and descendants, a connection to our ancestors is embedded in our genes. And sometimes, we stay connected through pain and fate, which may not be very smart, but we do it subconsciously.

Consequently, we don't allow ourselves to experience fortune and success. We assume that we would be betraying our ancestors if we were happier than them. It seems irrational to behave this way because such patterns are obviously harmful. But that is exactly what we do subconsciously. As long as these mechanisms operate undetected within us, we have no chance to reach our goals, as we are always preventing ourselves from doing so.

However, once we become aware of these mechanisms, we can transform and render them ineffective. They will no longer have any power over us.

Becoming aware will expand your consciousness Change can happen, and you will regain your power just as soon as you decide consciously to do so.

Self-Sabotage

There are several methods of self-sabotage. Some are evident, while others are more difficult to spot.

When things go wrong, we tend to blame others. But sometimes horrible things happen, and no one is to blame. Sure, some catastrophes are the result of someone else's actions, but this isn't always the case.

If you have a habit of blaming others, it might be worth looking into your role in the situation.

Let's say your partner exhibits certain problematic relationship behaviors that affect both of you. You determine they will not change and end your relationship with them. You're glad you broke up with them since their unwillingness to change prevented you from moving forward together. Your pals all agree that you made the proper decision.

But, according to clinical psychologist Maury Joseph, Psy.D., if you don't take the time to consider how you might have contributed to the troubles in that relationship, you're sabotaging your potential to learn and grow from it.

When things don't go as planned, you can choose to walk away. Moving on from settings that don't satisfy your needs is perfectly acceptable. At times, this may be the best alternative. However, it's usually a good idea to take a step back and assess whether or not you made a genuine attempt to succeed.

Perhaps you can't seem to hold onto a job for very long. You left one employment opportunity because your boss was unjust to you. Because of overstaffing, you were let go from a second job. You left your next job because of toxic employees, and so on.

These are all acceptable causes, but such an ongoing pattern could indicate something more. Doubts about your ability to thrive or keep steady employment may cause you to do things that impair your work performance or prevent success. Perhaps you're terrified of disagreements or criticism.

Procrastination

Have you ever become stuck or stalled while working on a critical task? You're not the only one!

You've prepped, done your research, and sat down to begin, only to find that you can't get started. Your motivation has completely vanished. So you clean out the refrigerator, organize your junk drawer, or start a movie marathon to escape the work.

Although procrastination might occur for no apparent reason, it usually has a root cause, such as:

- You're feeling overburdened by what you have to do and are having difficulties managing your time.
- You have doubts about your abilities or skills.
- Your task has created squabbles with friends or partners.

In various ways, you can subtly weaken yourself (and ruin your relationships) by procrastinating.

Maybe you're constantly up for a fight, even about minor matters, like who chose the last restaurant for dinner. Alternatively, you may purposefully "forget" significant occasions or make a mess in the kitchen to elicit reactions.

On the other hand, you may be easily offended or take things personally. Perhaps you find it difficult to express your emotions, especially when sad. So, instead of using more effective communication strategies, you turn to snark and passive aggression.

You're dating someone who isn't right for you.

Self-destructive actions are common in relationships. One sort of relationship self-sabotage is dating people who don't check all your boxes.

You could:

1. Continue to date people similar to you, even if your relationships typically fail.
2. Try to work things out with a partner who has very different future aspirations from you.
3. Stay in a relationship that isn't working.

Perhaps you're monogamous yet find yourself attracted to non-monogamous folks. You've tried non-monogamy before, but each time you've been disappointed and hurt. Or maybe you want children, but your partner does not. Everything else is going well, so you continue in the relationship, secretly hoping they will reconsider.

When we slip into these behaviors, we are hindering ourselves from discovering someone who is a better long-term match.

SELF-LIMITING BELIEFS

It's possible that self-limiting beliefs are the reason you've been attempting and failing to achieve certain goals that are important to you. Worse, you might not even be aware that you have these thoughts and have no clue how to change them.

If you're ready to take a significant step forward in attaining your goals, let's first learn more about limiting beliefs.

The assumptions or impressions you have about yourself, your circumstances, the future, and your ability to change that future are known as self-limiting beliefs. They are assumptions or ideas we have about ourself, the world, and our place in it. Such views are "self-limiting" in the sense that they prevent us from realizing our full potential.

The Formation of Self-Limiting Beliefs

The human mind is an odd contraption that can't seem to rest when one of the most important equations is missing. When we are presented with an issue but lack sufficient information, we tend to fill in the gaps by forming new beliefs.

A limiting belief's primary function can sometimes be to safeguard one's ego and self-worth. When a person fails to achieve their goals in life, their mind rapidly forms a limiting belief, such as "I am not lucky," to preserve their ego and make them feel better about themself.

Lack of knowledge is one of the primary causes of restricting beliefs. At one time in the distant past, thunder was thought to be caused by Zeus's rage. Humans thought Zeus was in the skies above, hurling thunderbolts with his hands. Needless to say, no rational person believes this today.

Limiting beliefs are usually formed when a person lacks sufficient understanding of a subject but insists on filling in the gaps regardless.

Common Self-Limiting Beliefs and Overcoming Methods

Here are six of the most frequent limiting beliefs that may be blocking you from manifesting, as well as some strategies for overcoming them.

1. "I don't think I'm good enough."

The underlying idea that you don't deserve the item you're seeking to manifest is possibly the most common limiting thought of all.

You won't attract love, money, a fulfilling profession, or anything else if you don't honestly believe you are good enough.

Instead, you'll send out a message to the universe that you don't expect to attract your goal.

Method to Overcome: Question your negative self-perceptions; where did they come from, and when did they begin? Make a list of reasons to reject them and review it every day.

2. "I require [this person's] approval."

When you focus on obtaining someone else's approval, you restrict yourself from accessing what you want out of life and restrict your mind from becoming who you really are.

Method to Overcome: The truth is that your authentic self will serve you best in life and will naturally attract the proper individuals; those who intuitively know and are drawn to your worth.

3. "There aren't enough resources to meet everyone's needs."

Do you ever feel compelled to seize something that belongs to you before someone else does? Alternatively, do you ever feel bad about getting what you want because you're afraid you're preventing someone else from receiving what they want?

In both circumstances, you're presuming that there's a limited supply of romance, riches, or success. And if you believe there isn't enough for everyone, you will begin to experience situations where there isn't enough!

Method to Overcome: Remind yourself that there is enough place in the universe for everyone to receive what they desire if they ask, believe, and work hard.

4. "I'm going to have to put in a lot of effort if I'm going to succeed."

Yes, whether or not you use the Law of Attraction, you must take actual steps to achieve your goals. However, if you believe that the only way to attain the life you want is to work yourself to death, you'll find that success is hard to come by without tremendous effort.

Method to Overcome: Strive for a balance; you must be motivated, ambitious, and willing to take proper action, but you will also benefit from understanding that you can attract success simply by thinking happy thoughts and enjoying your life.

5. "I have to suffer for others to be pleased."

While self-sacrifice is honorable and kind, if you suffer to the point where you cannot help yourself or others, you are ultimately undermining all of your aspirations. You'll likely burn out, feel lonely, and be overwhelmed.

Method to Overcome: Don't take on so much for others that you don't have any resources left to meet your own requirements.

If it's tough for you to focus on your own needs, set aside a time of the day that is solely dedicated to you. Use that hour to consider what will bring you happiness and rejuvenate your body and mind, and then do it!

If you increase your resilience in this way, you'll be better able to manifest your dreams (and help others manifest theirs).

6. "I need everything to fall into place perfectly."

Finally, many people new to the Law of Attraction have a predisposition toward setting an extremely specific purpose.

While it's essential to have a defined objective (e.g., losing three pounds rather than just "becoming healthy"), you run the risk of limiting your manifestation potential by making your aim too particular and regulated.

Method to Overcome: Focus on one goal, such as "attracting a relationship with person X," rather than many goals, such as "attracting a phone call from X" and "meeting X next week."

Once you've set your intention, be open to it manifesting in a variety of ways, and keep an eye out for indicators that your life is altering in unexpected ways!

Re-Programming Self-Limiting Beliefs

The thoughts (or stories) we have about ourselves are our beliefs.

The fascinating aspect of beliefs is that we are not born with them. As soon as we are born, they begin to develop. Our parents, grandparents, instructors, siblings, boyfriends, and friends influence our beliefs. Then, as we grow older and travel through life, we form our own new ideas, replacing some of the old ones while maintaining a firm grip on others from our youth, some of which aren't benefitting us at all!

If your parents yelled and screamed at you and told you, "You can't do that," you're in trouble. Alternatively, if they made you feel like a bad child or that making mistakes is bad, those beliefs are embedded in your belief system, and unless you re-program them, they will limit your level of confidence.

Your beliefs have an impact on that negative voice in your head that tells you things like, "I'm not good enough" and "I can't do it." Or "I'm not intelligent enough," "I'm not deserving of that," and "I'm not likable."

Many people are all too familiar with these kinds of thoughts, and frequently repeat negative comments in their heads without even realizing it. This causes only destructive emotions and problems.

We must have good, empowering attitudes about ourselves. Positive beliefs lead to positive feelings, while negative (limiting) beliefs lead to negative emotions. And our beliefs influence our ideas and emotions. What you believe determines how you feel.

You will be successful at your new work if you believe you will be.

You will not be successful if you believe you are not good enough or your boss dislikes you.

In either case, what you choose to think will become your reality. It's 100 percent true, and it's one of the universe's 12 laws!

Having these self-doubting ideas (limited beliefs) prevents you from progressing. Because beliefs always come true, you must have positive views and thoughts about overcoming your insecurities, because if you feel you will never conquer them, you can be sure you never will.

Your Thoughts Become Your Beliefs.

Your words are made up of your thoughts.

Your words are translated into actions.

Your actions determine your outcomes.

Because we all act based on our beliefs, our beliefs directly impact our behavior. We will naturally limit our actions if we hold self-limiting ideas about our ability to achieve high levels of confidence, happiness, and success. If we limit the actions we take, we will only have so much confidence, joy, and success.

"It's just who I am" or "I hear it all the time, so it must be real" are common thoughts. But if you have these thoughts, you're holding yourself hostage in your own comfort zone, enslaved by your worries. Many people devote far too much time and energy to maintaining and defending their restricting and fear-based ideas.

Change your thoughts, and you'll change your life!

There are numerous ways to re-program your mind and arrive at a powerful, positive frame of mind, escaping fear and uncertainty. My personal top three techniques are as follows:

1.) **EFT tapping** is one of my favorite techniques for realizing FAST (nearly instant) outcomes. It stands for Emotional Freedom Technique, and it entails tapping on specific meridian points while uttering specific words and affirmations (the most important of which is, "Even though (insert limiting belief here), I choose to love, honor, and accept myself."

This technique enables you to process negative ideas or unpleasant feelings, accept yourself as you are, and GROW into the best version of your most authentic self.

2.) Spending at least 10-15 minutes each day **meditating**. You don't need to be an expert at meditating. Many people claim they "don't know how" or that they "can't focus or clear their minds." First and foremost, you DO know how because you probably already do it in various ways without even realizing it (in the shower, when you fall asleep, etc.). In some ways, it's akin to daydreaming. Second, it's perfectly normal to have a lot of thoughts, especially when you're first starting, but the goal is to practice letting those thoughts go and focus on your breathing. You will become more proficient at this as you practice.

Meditating offers numerous advantages, such as providing relaxation, gaining greater clarity and motivation, reducing stress, and improving mood and vitality. It allows us to quiet our mind so we can connect with our higher self and align more readily with our truth. Just make sure you're in a quiet place where you won't be disturbed.

3.) **Affirmations** are quite effective! I recommend writing them down, over and over, until they are imprinted in your subconscious thinking. Make a list of affirmations that feel particularly nice to you. Aside from writing them down, pay attention to when you DO hear your negative self-talk and say "STOP," then repeat the opposing affirmation to yourself.

If you start to feel or hear the thought "I never have enough," you can say "STOP" and say something like, "I always have enough. There is always more than enough available for me. There will always be enough. I am always supported. New opportunities are always coming my way. I deserve it. I am worthy of abundance. Everything always works out for me." You will likely notice a shift in your perspective just by reading that. It has a lot of power. And with practice, you'll begin to get into the flow of those words and accept them as fact, which is a good thing.

How Limiting Beliefs Affect Behavior

Everyone's potential is limited by their beliefs: Limiting beliefs have an impact on behavior, since they prevent us from doing specific activities that we would have done if the belief didn't exist. If an intelligent child believes he is not intelligent, he may never study and will flunk the exams.

Filtering information and beliefs: As discussed earlier, we filter information depending on our views and only absorb information aligned with our beliefs. This impacts our conduct, since it biases us toward what we believe, regardless of information to the contrary. That is why it is difficult to get someone to believe in something that contradicts their ideas.

Reality is shaped by beliefs: If someone believes they will never find work (belief), they will not be motivated to prepare for the job market (change in behavior), and they will fail when they try to find work (so their belief will become true). This is how beliefs influence reality.

Self-confidence and self-belief: Self-confidence is nothing more than a set of beliefs about oneself. If your beliefs are positive, you will act confidently.

What can be learned from the link between conduct and beliefs?

It is evident that our beliefs can influence our actions, behavior, and potential. If we learn how to develop positive beliefs and get rid of negative ones, we can harness their immense power to be on our side.

There is no limit to what we can achieve in this world if we have a positive and powerful belief system.

7

LIVING THE LAW OF ATTRACTION

If you are tired of life and are looking for a way to change it, yet you have no idea how exactly to go about it, consider the Law of Attraction. It can give you both control and freedom to reshape your life as desired.

For those who want success, financial abundance, good health, and happiness, you are in the right place. The Law of Attraction exercises change how you think and feel and will improve every aspect of your life.

When you work hard for your goals, and they still prove to be beyond your reach, the solution lies in this unique universal law.

Nevertheless, applying the Law of Attraction is not always as easy as people think. For this reason, I want to introduce you to some exercises that will help you effectively realize your goals and dreams.

These exercises are meant to help you become the kind of person who can commit and believe in this universal law.

One good thing about humans is that we are habitual creatures, which means that the more you do these exercises, the more they become a part of you and will work to increase your positivity—which is what the Law of Attraction requires.

THE POWER OF A MORNING AND EVENING ROUTINE

Having a morning and evening routine has changed my life. It doesn't matter what time you go to bed or wake up in the morning. The important thing is a structured ritual you consistently go through each morning and evening.

Morning Ritual

Have you ever gotten out of bed with only a few minutes to shower, get dressed, and eat breakfast before you had to run out the door so you wouldn't be late for work? You're not the only one. That's how many people spend their mornings - rushing around.

A morning ritual gives you time to yourself before you honor any other commitments, like taking care of your family or going to work. By waking up thirty minutes to an hour before you normally start your day, you've carved out some time that's just for you.

Examples of things you can include in your morning ritual include:

- Meditation
- Showering
- Gratitude
- Reviewing your goals
- Yoga

- Eating a healthy breakfast
- Reading
- Going to the gym
- Stretching
- Going for a run

Evening Ritual

Adding an evening ritual to my day has helped me wind down, enabling me to get a good night's sleep. About an hour before you go to sleep, spend some time on yourself.

Examples of things you can include in your evening ritual include:

- Journaling
- Going over the day's successes
- Having a bath
- Meditating
- Reading
- Drinking herbal tea
- Visualizing what you want as you read over your goals

Meditation

Meditation is another powerful tool that you can use to attract more of what you want into your life. When you meditate, you quiet the mind and clear it of excessive thoughts. You will begin to notice what thoughts you're having that might be preventing you from effectively using the Law of Attraction, and your vibration will rise when you've calmed your mind.

Another benefit of meditation is that it shows you that you are in control of your thoughts. Sometimes, when your mind is racing and you have many thoughts coming into your head, it can be challenging to control them and avoid negative thinking.

Practicing meditation daily will help you learn to control your thoughts.

Commit to making meditation a habit. You can add it to your morning or evening routine. Many people enjoy meditating first thing in the morning, while others find it a relaxing way to end their day.

Start by sitting quietly with your legs crossed, breathing in deeply through your nose, and exhaling through your mouth. Focus on each breath.

You can meditate for just ten minutes when you're starting, and it will still be hugely beneficial to you. As you improve, you can increase your time every day to twenty or thirty minutes, and eventually to an hour.

If you have trouble clearing your head, try a guided meditation. Listening to someone's calming voice with gentle background music can make a big difference.

5 GOALS A DAY KEEPS THE UNIVERSE AT BAY

If you've read any self-development books, then you've probably heard about the importance of setting goals, which ties in nicely with the Law of Attraction. When you create goals for yourself, you're clarifying what you want and when you want it.

If you want to lose weight, then you could set a goal like this one and write it in your journal:

- I will easily lose twenty pounds by December 31st of this year by eating healthy foods and exercising daily.

If you want to earn more money, then you could set a goal like this one:

- I will easily earn $100,000 a year by December 31st of this year by looking for new opportunities that will help me grow my income.

You've set a clear intention by writing down a specific goal along with a date that it must be completed.

Write this goal down at least once every day. I like to start and end the day by writing down my goals.

By writing your goals daily, you're focusing your subconscious mind on them. This is where the Law of Attraction comes in. Your subconscious mind can't tell what's real and what's not. Your subconscious mind accepts everything that it's given. If you're telling your subconscious mind that you're going to lose twenty pounds by a specific date, it's going to become programmed into your mind.

REPEAT POSITIVE AFFIRMATIONS

Now that you know what you want to attract and you've created a few goals, you can begin using affirmations to build the belief that these things can really happen.

Affirmations should be used daily. I like to use them when I'm sitting in traffic or waiting in a line. I have 3-5 affirmations that I know of by heart that I can say to myself whenever I have a few moments, or I find that my mind is distracted.

These are my favorite affirmations:

1. I can do anything that I set my mind to.
2. I am living a life that is full of abundance.

3. I love and accept myself for who I am.
4. Visualization comes naturally to me.
5. I attract money naturally.

Search online for affirmations or come up with a few of your own.

Take the time to write down 3-5 affirmations that you can easily remember and use daily.

Choose the best way to use these affirmations:

- Say them in front of the mirror as you're getting ready in the morning.
- Write them down in your journal.
- Write them on a post-it and stick them next to your computer where you will see them every day.
- Carry them with you in your purse or wallet and say them to yourself throughout the day.

ATTITUDE OF GRATITUDE

Being thankful for what you have is a powerful habit to develop. If I could give you one piece of advice to take away with you, it would be to be grateful for everything you have and to remind yourself of all of those things every day.

What are you grateful for?

No matter what situation you're in, you can find something to be grateful for. It might be the smallest thing that most people wouldn't even consider acknowledging or being thankful for, like the ray of sunshine that's warming your face.

Things you can be grateful for:

- I am grateful that I am alive today.

- I am grateful for my health.
- I am grateful for my pets who love me unconditionally.
- I am grateful for the electricity that lights my home.
- I am grateful for the roads that make traveling easy.
- I am grateful for the food that I've eaten today.
- I am grateful to have a roof over my head.

In a journal, record three things you are grateful for every day. You can do this in the morning or at night just before you go to bed. If you make this exercise a habit, it will supercharge your manifesting skills.

Try not to repeat the things you are grateful for. By challenging yourself to think of three new things every day, you'll become more aware of all the little things you have to be thankful for.

CREATE A VISION BOARD

Many of you have probably heard of vision boards. When used correctly, vision boards can speed up the manifestation process.

Vision boards are a collage of images, words, and ideas that inspire you. These are the things that you want in your life. Vision boards can be digital, or you can find images in magazines to create a physical board that you can hang up on your wall.

One of the most common mistakes you can make with vision boards is to spend an hour or two making one and thinking that everything you put on your board is now going to magically come to you. Vision boards are a wonderful tool, but remember that there's still work involved to make your dreams come to life.

I have my vision board on the wall above my computer. Whenever I sit down to work, I look up and see what I'm working for.

Seeing those images daily means that I am constantly focusing on them.

I look up at my vision board several times a day and think about going on that vacation or living in that dream home.

Vision boards help keep your dreams at the forefront of your attention. That attention and obsession with what you want will allow you to manifest your goals faster. Your vision board should inspire you to keep working on your goals and continue to progress toward the result.

Find pictures representing your dreams and the experiences you want to have in your life and use them on your vision board. If you're doing a physical vision board, gather old magazines from friends and family. Cut out words and pictures that will excite you and keep you moving toward your goals.

SIGNS THE LAW OF ATTRACTION IS WORKING FOR YOU

1. You recognize your Emotional Guidance System.

One of the most important things you can learn about is your emotional guidance system (EGS). You'll be able to maintain yourself in line with what you want if you start to become aware of how you feel about your goal.

If you feel good when you see others in happy relationships, for example, your emotional guidance system is signaling you that you're on the right track.

If you want to use the Law of Attraction to materialize a loving relationship, but you're feeling horrible because you become envious whenever you see a happy couple walking hand in hand in love, that's your EGS telling you that you're out of alignment and need to get back on track.

When you find yourself feeling unpleasant, give thanks that your emotional guidance system operates well and then work on raising your vibration around that new companion you seek.

To boost your vibration, you must begin focusing solely on the things you desire and the reasons why you CAN get them. It may take some time, but you will ultimately convert those negative thoughts to more positive ones, and you will begin to vibrate in tune with what you want.

2. When you think of your desires, you feel good.

This sign is a continuation of the previous one. Feeling well indicates that you are on track to achieve your goals.

Like a magnet, your vibrations attract what you desire, so you invite that desire into your life when you feel good and vibrate in tune with what you want.

I prefer to stop what I'm doing when I feel good about something I desire, appreciate the sensation, and feed into the positive vibration.

3. You notice indicators.

Indicators are small signs that the things you wish to manifest are beginning to arrive in your life.

For example, if you want more money, start looking for small items, such as a $10 bill, maybe from a friend who paid you back for something.

If you go to buy something you were planning to buy anyway, such as a new coat, and it's $40 off, you'll end up with $40 more in your pocket than you planned.

You may begin to notice these small indicators that there's plenty of what you desire all around you.

4. Synchronicities will occur.

These are strong indicators that the Law of Attraction operates in your favor.

When unexpected people or conditions appear that you need in order to make your desire a reality, you know you're on the right track.

For instance, you might want to write a book but don't know where to begin.

The next day, as you're driving home, your partner calls and asks if you could pick up some milk. You stop at a random store to get milk, and as you walk out, you spot a note on the pin-up board near the exit offering beginner writing classes. You enroll in the course, and the rest is history.

5. You notice increased sensitivity to your desires.

Let's say you desire a new Mercedes. You've decided on the exact model and color you want, and you've made it clear that you wish to receive that automobile as soon as possible.

Then, as if by magic, you begin to see that car everywhere. You've gone from seeing them occasionally to seeing them ALL THE TIME.

Well, the same thing can happen with whatever you desire. If you begin to see and hear more about your want, this means it is drawn to you because it is on your vibrational frequency.

Maybe you overhear conversations regarding your desire. Or you listen to a radio broadcaster discuss it. All of these are evidence that the Law of Attraction is operating in your favor.

6. You're excited.

Feeling pleased and anticipating the manifestation of your wish is a sign that the Law of Attraction is working for you. If you didn't think you'd get what you desired, you wouldn't be excited. It's because you expect it to happen that you're delighted.

Feeling enthusiastic signals to the universe that you're looking forward to acquiring what you want, and the universe will respond by giving it to you, often in unexpected ways!

IMPORTANT LAW OF ATTRACTION QUOTES TO LIVE BY

Reading quotes about the Law of Attraction can help you internalize what it is all about. Such things can motivate you just as you are about to give up, especially when you think it's not working for you anymore.

"It is the combination of thought and love which forms the irresistible force of the Law of Attraction."

- Charles Hammel

"Think the thought until you believe it, and once you believe it, it is."

- Abraham Hicks

"Thoughts become things. If you see it in your mind, you will hold it in your hand."

- Bob Proctor

"Your whole life is a manifestation of the thoughts that go on in your head."

- Lisa Nichols

"See the things that you want as already yours. Know that they will come to you at need. Then let them come. Don't fret and worry about them. Don't think about your lack of them. Think of them as yours, belonging to you, as already in your possession."

- Robert Collier

"The Law of Attraction states that whatever you focus on, think about, read about, and talk about intensely, you're going to attract more of into your life."

- Jack Canfield

"To live your greatest life, you must first become a leader within yourself. Take charge of your life, begin attracting and manifesting all that you desire in life."

- Sonia Ricotti

"Eliminate all doubt and replace it with the full expectation that you will receive what you are asking for."

- Rhonda Byrne

"Most people are thinking about what they don't want, and they're wondering why it shows up over and over again."

- John Assaraf

"The Universe likes speed. Don't delay, don't second-guess, don't doubt."

- The Secret

"To bring anything into your life, imagine that it's already there."

- Richard Bach

"Whatever the mind can conceive, it can achieve."

- W. Clement Stone

"See yourself living in abundance, and you will attract it."

- Rhonda Byrne

"You already have within you everything you need to turn your dreams into reality."

- Wallace D. Wattles

"Gratitude is an attitude that hooks us up to our source of supply. And the more grateful you are, the closer you become to your Maker, to the architect of the Universe, to the spiritual core of your being. It's a phenomenal lesson."

- Bob Proctor

"Nurture great thoughts, for you will never go higher than your thoughts."

- Benjamin Disraeli

"A person is only limited by the thoughts that he chooses."

- James Allen

"We receive exactly what we expect to receive."

- John Holland

"Once you replace negative thoughts with positive ones, you'll start having positive results."

- Willie Nelson

"Look forward to where you want to be and spend no time complaining about where you are."

- Esther Hicks

"You create your own universe as you go along."

- Winston Churchill

CONCLUSION

Everyone has at least one moment in their lives when they feel like everything is spinning out of their control financially, professionally, physically, socially, or emotionally. The good news is, no matter how far you fall, you can achieve your goals. Now that you've read this book, you should have more motivation to do just that.

With your deeper understanding of the Law of Attraction, you can use it to manifest all you desire in life. Through concrete examples, this book has shown you how to use the Law of Attraction to reach your goals, whether to improve your relationships, your finances, boost your health, cultivate confidence, achieve success, or enjoy a spiritual awakening.

If you need to make sure you're doing it right, go back to the discussion about how the law works. When you start, you might need to practice seeing the positive side of things, but use the tips in this book until you make it a habit. To be more effective at using the law to your advantage, we've also shown you the importance of meditation.

Hopefully, you now recognize the power of affirmations and how best to do them. Remember, it's not just about saying the words, but making sure that they ring true for you. We've learned the importance of deciding what you want, asking for it, not blaming anyone or anything for whatever happens in your life, being open to possibilities, and staying persistent.

Included in this book are many quotes that you can print, save on your phone, or use as a desktop screensaver to provide you with everyday encouragement to continue practicing the techniques of the Law of Attraction.

There is no better time than right now to start taking the proper steps to manifest all your dreams. I hope you will use this book as a guide for making the Law of Attraction work for you, as you manifest your deepest desires.